ENDORSEMENTS

Pastor Kynan T. Bridges, in his profound book, *The Power of Unlimited Faith,* immerses the believer with the concept of living in God's kingdom through believing and renewing one's mind with the creative power of God's Word. When faith dwells in our hearts, the invisible realm, which is the truer reality than the natural realm, comes to life. *The Power of Unlimited Faith* empowers the reader to be spiritually transformed to see past the natural realms of limitations by entering into the invisible realms where God has chosen in His sovereignty to cloak Himself. Faith removes the boundaries of the expected realm so we are able to experience the supernatural moves of God. Faith enables people to overcome a belief system that says, "If I see physical proof or natural evidence then I will believe it is possible." Unlimited faith is a truth that God has given His church to unlock the fullness of His Word to look beyond the current temporary circumstance to possess God's eternal promises for our lives.

Dr. Barbie L. Breathitt, PhD
Breath of the Spirit Ministries
Author of *Dream Encounters,* www.MyOnar.com
Gateway to the Seer Realm, www.BarbieBreathitt.com

Kynan Bridges is one of my favorite Bible teachers. We are on the precipice of the greatest revival and move of miracles in history. This book will prepare you to enter the last act of the last play!

Sid Roth
Host, *It's Supernatural!*

Kynan Bridges stirs up a passion and hunger within the heart of the believer to long for and see the glory of God! In his latest book, *The Power of Unlimited Faith*, Kynan prepares the body of Christ to get ready to see this All-Powerful God work in our lives and manifest His glory and kingdom.

DR. JEREMY LOPEZ
CEO, Indentitynetwork.net

In this exciting new book, *The Power of Unlimited Faith*, Kynan Bridges simplifies faith. Through this book you will gain a practical understanding of how to live a life of victory, a life of the miraculous, and walk in the supernatural power of God every day. Kynan Bridges shows you the time-tested biblical secrets to following in the footsteps of Jesus. Get ready to be challenged by this book to expect and experience more. Get ready to take the brakes off and walk in Unlimited Faith.

PASTOR GLORIA E. BRIDGES
Ministry Director
Grace & Peace Global Fellowship Church

THE POWER OF
UNLIMITED FAITH

THE POWER OF
UNLIMITED FAITH

LIVING IN THE MIRACULOUS EVERYDAY
KYNAN BRIDGES

DESTINY IMAGE® PUBLISHERS, INC.

P.O. Box 310, Shippensburg, PA 17257-0310

"Promoting Inspired Lives."

This book and all other Destiny Image and Destiny Image Fiction books are available at Christian bookstores and distributors worldwide.

For more information on foreign distributors, call 717-532-3040.

Reach us on the Internet: www.destinyimage.com.

Cover Design by River Publishing

ISBN 13 TP: 978-0-7684-0465-4

ISBN 13 Ebook: 978-0-7684-0466-1

For Worldwide Distribution, Printed in the U.S.A.

1 2 3 4 5 6 7 8 / 18 17 16 15 14

DEDICATION

I dedicate this book to the Lord Jesus Christ, the King of kings and Lord of lords. I also dedicate it to Gloria Bridges—my lovely and virtuous wife, the mother of my three beautiful children (Ella, Naomi, and Isaac), and my number one supporter in life and ministry; I love you more than words can express. To my church family (Grace & Peace Global Fellowship), who have been instrumental in praying for and supporting this project—God bless you!

ACKNOWLEDGMENTS

First of all, I want to take a moment and acknowledge my precious Lord Jesus Christ. It is through Him that I am able to write this and all books. To my wife and ministerial staff, thank you! To my parents James and Juanita Bridges—I honor you. To Destiny Image Publishers, thank you for believing in me and helping to release this message to the body of Christ. Special thanks to the production and editing team including: Ronda Ranalli, Terri Meckes, Dominique Abney, Mykela Krieg, and Isheka Harrison (my staff editor), to name a few.

I also want to take a moment and acknowledge great men and women of the faith who have impacted my life and ministry in a positive way (either directly or indirectly) including: Pastor Wayne C. Thompson, Dr. Mark Chironna, Derek Prince, Smith Wigglesworth, John G. Lake, Oswald Chambers, John Wesley, Jack Coe, Oral Roberts, Kathryn Kuhlman, R.W. Shambach, Kenneth E. Hagin, Dr. T.L. Osborn, Dr. Martin Luther King Jr., Heidi Baker, Bill Johnson, Randy Clark, Mahesh and Bonnie Chavda, Hank and Brenda Kunneman, Apostle G. Maldanado, Sid Roth, Rabbi Jonathan Bernis, Dr. Cindy Trimm, Apostle Charles Ndifon, Dr. Charles and Francis Hunter, Joan Hunter, Pastor Marlin D. Harris, Dr. E.V. Hill, Dr. Barbie Breathitt, Mike Bickle, Pastor Andre Mitchell, Apostle Mark

T. Jones, Marilyn Hickey, Pastor Tony Kemp, John Loren Sanford, Dr. T.L. Lowery, Dr. Douglas Wingate, Benny Hinn, and Evangelist Reinhard Bonnke. Thank you for your service and gift to the body of Christ.

God bless you!

CONTENTS

PREFACE

THIS MAY BE ONE OF THE MOST IMPORTANT BOOKS I HAVE WRITTEN thus far. Why? In my many years of being a believer in Jesus, I have found that nothing is more fundamental to our Christian experience than faith. In fact, the Bible says that without faith, it is impossible to please God. Consequently, no subject has been more confusing, more marred with misunderstanding, and more abused than the subject of faith. It is my sincere conviction that if we are going to experience the power and presence of God that He longs to manifest in this generation, we must have a solid biblical grasp of this wonderful truth.

I can remember a time in my life when I was not experiencing victory the way the Bible reveals; I was so frustrated. Little did I know that the problem was my own wrong belief system and not God. I was full of doubt, unbelief, and fear. "Lord, why can't I experience the miracles I read about?" The answer to this question and many others is contained within the pages of this book.

Faith is the key to releasing God's supernatural power in your life. It is the means by which you and I will come to live in the miraculous every day. Can living in the miraculous daily be possible? "YES!" Many of you reading this book have something stirring deep within your spirit. It is a godly discontentment. It is a desire to experience more! This feeling is not unique to you; the Holy Spirit is orchestrating this apparent phenomenon. God is bringing us back to a victorious and biblical understanding of faith—*unlimited faith!*

You will be challenged, encouraged, and most importantly you will be empowered as you read and carefully consider the contents of this book. May Christ be glorified in you and may your faith go to another level—as you embrace the endless possibilities revealed in the Word of God.

God bless you!

IN THE BEGINNING

In the beginning was the Word, and the Word was with God, and the Word was God. He was in the beginning with God. All things were made through Him, and without Him nothing was made that was made. In Him was life, and the life was the light of men. And the light shines in the darkness, and the darkness did not comprehend it (JOHN 1:1-5).

THE HOLY SPIRIT IS MOVING MIGHTILY IN THE DAYS IN WHICH WE live. Men, women, and children are experiencing a hunger and thirst for God's presence and power like never before. All around the world we are seeing revival and reformation. What is happening? There is a godly discontent for mundane and lifeless Christianity. The Bible gives endless accounts of miracles such as the sick being healed, blind eyes opening, storms being rebuked, lepers being cleansed, and men walking on water; yet the modern church at large has seemed to neglect these realities in our preaching and teaching. For many in the body of Christ, these types of occurrences are the substance of great myths, but for countless others there is a cry to experience the very miracles we read about in the Bible.

I, like many of you reading this book, am desperate to experience the power and presence of God. The Bible portrays a God capable of so much more than Sunday sermons and small group meetings. He was and is a God who consistently displays His might and splendor from the beginning of time until now. What is the catalyst for this awesome demonstration of God's omnipotence? More importantly, what do ancient biblical accounts of the miraculous have to do with us today?

I want to present to you a very powerful yet misunderstood word: faith. Most of us are very familiar with the word *faith*. After all, faith in Jesus Christ is what makes you and I children of God. But, what does this word really mean? Is it some mystical power to name and claim the things you desire; is it a philosophical idea debated in seminary schools, or could it be so much more?

The truth is that every believer in Christ is called to live a life of faith: *unlimited faith* to be more exact. Through faith, seemingly ordinary men and women have healed the sick, raised the dead to life, and even transformed their generations for the glory of God. These average people were able to witness miraculous displays of God. They, as you and I will soon discover, realized the supernatural power of God in their lives by making the simple decision to believe for the impossible (to exercise faith).

 I believe that faith is the key to experiencing the miraculous power of God in our daily lives; we too can encounter the realities of the supernatural.

Why is this topic so important? God is desperate to pour out the fullness of His glory in this hour. He wants the world to see how real He is. This can only be realized when you and I live the Christian life as it was originally intended. When we speak of the Christian life, we are not talking about a religious experience; we are speaking of so much more! What if we could do the same works that Jesus did right now? What if we could live in the miraculous today? What if we could live in a higher dimension of power, victory, and manifestation, here and now?

I believe that faith is the key to experiencing the miraculous power of God in our daily lives; we too can encounter the realities of the supernatural. Before we investigate these realities further, let us start from the very beginning in order to grasp what unlimited faith is all about.

THE BASIS FOR FAITH

I remember when I first became a Christian. What a wonderful experience! I was instantly healed and delivered of chronic loneliness and depression, and for the first time in my life I had a sense of purpose and worth. One of the first things I remember doing as a new believer was developing a habit of regular Bible reading. In fact, I read the Bible several hours a day. Much of what I read, I did not even understand, but that did not deter me from my quest to digest all the knowledge of God that I possibly could. I figured that if I wanted to understand God, the best way to go about that task would be to read the Bible.

One of the first verses I read was John 1:1. This later became one of my favorite scriptures. In this verse, the Bible tells us that in the very beginning of creation *was* the Word. What in heaven does this mean? I came to discover from my personal studies that the Greek noun used for "word" is *logos* (Strong's G3056). This is probably one of the more sophisticated words in the Greek language. It conveys the idea of a thought, concept, or expression. Another way of putting it is: that which gives form and purpose to the tangible universe. As

I read more and more, the strangest thing took place; a light bulb went off in my spirit. I realized in that moment that everything in the Kingdom of God rises and falls on the Word of God—especially faith. In fact, I have come to discover that the Word of God is the key to having faith in God. The Word of God created all that we can see in the natural realm. Hebrews 11:3 says this:

> *By faith we understand that the worlds were framed by the word of God, so that the things which are seen were not made of things which are visible.*

This is one of the most powerful scriptures in the Bible. In it, we see that the Word of God *framed* the very worlds. What does that mean? When the Bible speaks of worlds (plural) it is referring to the ages. It comes from the Greek word *aion* (Strong's G165) and it literally means "unbroken age," "perpetuity of time," or universe. The word *framed* means to render, to repair, or to establish. Simply put, God's Word created all that we know in time and space and established order in the midst of chaos. The very universe itself was set into motion by the spoken Word of God. Scientists are still baffled at the causes and effects of creation. Astrophysicists have postulated what is known as the *oscillating universe theory*, which suggests that the universe as we know it has continued to expand over the ages through one profound event.

Well, it is not a mystery. The Bible already tells us what that single event was: creation. In Genesis 1:1-3, the Bible tells us that, "In the beginning God created the heavens and the earth. The earth was without form, and void; and darkness was on the face of the deep... Then God said, 'Let there be light.'" The moment God spoke those Words, He set in motion spiritual forces that would, in turn, establish the very physical universe. The whole of what we know about God and creation is a by-product of the Word of God. What does this mean to you and I as believers? Furthermore, what does any of this have to do with faith? It means that if we are going to operate in faith, we must understand the basis for all faith, which is the Word of God. In fact, the more we understand the Word of God, the more that Word will release the power of unlimited faith in our lives.

GOD SAID!

The purpose of this book is to teach you the very practical keys to walking in faith and to enable you to release the supernatural power that faith has in your everyday life. Many people have asked the questions: "Is it possible for everyday people to walk in signs, wonders, and miracles?" "Can everyday people be used of God to do the impossible?" The answer to these questions is a resilient "YES!" In my studies of God's Word over the years, I have found that the Bible is filled with accounts of everyday people who simply learned to take God at His Word. Some of these people were so ordinary and average that you probably would not even recognize them today. What allowed these people to experience the miraculous power of God on a consistent basis? The common denominator of all the biblical examples we have is one thing: *a right response to something God said.*

In my opinion, this is one of the simplest definitions of faith: *a positive response to what God says.* We see this in the life of Abraham in Genesis chapter 12, verse 1, when God told him to leave his family and his country. What a challenging instruction. How does a person leave all that he is familiar with to go and follow a voice he has never heard before? The first thing that Abraham had to do was believe that the voice speaking to him was the voice of the Almighty God. In other words, he was responding to what God said.

This is the key to releasing God's supernatural power in our lives. This is the secret to living in the dimension of the miraculous every day. You and I have to be convinced of what God has already said and respond accordingly.

THE WORD IS FULL OF *SUPERNATURAL POWER*

Throughout my life and ministry I have personally experienced many phenomenal miracles. I have seen the sick healed and the lame walk. I have seen God's miraculous provision. I have seen signs and wonders. The question remains whether this phenomenon is relegated to high profile ministers and personalities, or if this power is available to every believer in Jesus Christ.

I believe that we all should experience the Bible in a very practical way. Why? Because God said we can. The moment God spoke the earth into being and said, *"Let there be light,"* He was giving every one of His children an invitation to access His power through His Word. The more you and I meditate upon the Word, the more the Word releases supernatural power. The Bible says that God said, "Let there be light." This statement in the original Hebrew language literally means to come into being or to appear (literally: light be!). The implication is that the light that needed to be manifested was already contained inside the Word of God.

Every miracle begins with the Word. If you wantto experience miracles in your life, it must begin with the Word.

I discovered this concept early on in my Christian life and it has radically transformed my relationship with God. I realized that the Word of God is pregnant with the miracle working power of God. If you want to gain access to miracle working power, you must first gain access to the Word. The interesting thing about this is that most

Christians spend very little time studying the Word of God on a regular basis. There is a cry throughout America for a move of God's Spirit, but every move of God recorded in the Bible is connected with God's Word. Every miracle begins with the Word. If you want to experience miracles in your life, it must begin with the Word. Later we will talk about the details of faith, but I want to spend a little more time talking about the profound power of God's Word.

THE WORD GIVES FORM AND PURPOSE

Before you and I came to Christ, like the earth referenced in Genesis 1, we were without form and void. What does this mean? The word for "without form" is the Hebrew word *tohuw* (Strong's H8414) and it literally means formlessness, confusion, and emptiness. This doesn't sound good at all does it? Not only were we without form, but we were also void. What does this mean? The word "void" comes from the Hebrew word *bohuw* (Strong's H922), which means emptiness and waste. Without being connected to the Creator, all we can produce is emptiness and confusion, but once we come into fellowship with Him through Jesus Christ, things are supposed to change.

How does this change take place in us? The Bible says in Genesis 1:3, "Then God said...." In order to set things the way He intended, God spoke to the chaos and the confusion in our lives and said let there be light. Without God's Word, nothing in our lives has purpose and meaning; but with the Word, our lives have unlimited capacity. It alone is the only means to releasing God's original intent into our lives. There are so many believers in the body of Christ today who are not tapping into their unlimited potential.

The Word of God is what gives form and purpose to your life. There is no substitute. You may say, "I didn't think the Word was that important." Well, it absolutely is! Why? Before the Word was spoken there was nothing but chaos and darkness. I want to reiterate the fact that the miracle working power of God is contained within the Word of God. The Bible says in 2 Corinthians 4:6:

> *For it is the God who commanded light to shine out of darkness, who has shone in our hearts to give the light of the knowledge of the glory of God in the face of Jesus Christ.*

God called the light out of the darkness in the beginning of creation, and the Bible says that He did the same thing inside of our hearts when we gave our lives to Him. This light reveals the glory of God. The moment God said, "Let there be light," He released eternal light that would continue to illuminate all of creation. This very light is what shines inside the heart of every born-again believer. This light brings the knowledge of the Glory of God in the face of Jesus Christ. What does that mean? It means that the Word of God tells us all that we need to know about our heavenly Father. The Word gives us access to the very Glory of God.

Isn't this the prayer of many in the body of Christ, "God, show us Your glory"? We write songs about it, go to conferences about it, and even write books about the glory. The truth is, the Glory of God (according to scripture) is revealed by the Word. Do you want to live a life filled with God's miraculous power? Do you want to experience signs, wonders, and miracles every day? Do you want to release the supernatural power of God through unlimited faith? It all begins with us developing a hunger and a thirst for the Word of God and applying that Word to every single situation in our lives.

THE SPIRIT AND THE WORD

From the very beginning of creation, there has been an inseparable connection between God's Spirit and God's Word. The Bible says in Genesis 1:2 that the Spirit of God moved over the face of the waters. The word *moved* means to hover or to brood. Before God said anything, His Spirit was already moving. I believe this is in the Bible to show us the sovereign relationship between the Word and the Spirit. You cannot have one without the other. We cannot walk in the power of God without the Word of God, and the Word of God will always manifest the power of God's Spirit.

Why is this so important? It is critical to understand the basis for living in the realm of the Spirit. When we realize that everything begins with the Word, then we can start to use the Word to begin living the life that God intended—a life saturated with the miraculous. Jesus said in John 6:63, "It is the Spirit who gives life; the flesh profits nothing. The words that I speak to you are spirit, and they are life." What did Jesus mean when He said this? The word translated "spirit" is the Greek word *pneuma* (Strong's G4151), which is literally referring to the Holy Spirit (the third person of the Trinity). Here we see that Jesus equates His Words with the very person of the Holy Spirit. Wow! This is amazing!

The same Spirit of God that was present in the beginning of the creation is the same Spirit that impregnated the Words of Jesus and manifested the very life of God in those who heard it.

However, He did not stop by equating His words with the Spirit; He also says they are life. What does this mean? This is the Greek word *zoe* (Strong's G2222), which is literally "the absolute fullness of life," "life real and genuine," "the life of God." Simply put, this "life" is referring to the very life God has in Himself. It is eternal life. So we see then that Jesus's words (the Word of God) were not just principles and precepts to live by, but they were the very Spirit of God being released through the Word. This is why you and I must develop a deeper delight in God's Word if we want to experience the supernatural.

The same Spirit of God that was present in the beginning of the creation is the same Spirit that impregnated the Words of Jesus and manifested the very life of God in those who heard it. What a wonderful truth! Simply put, possessing unlimited faith (faith for the miraculous) begins with recognition of the unlimited power of God's Word. As you read this book, you will learn what faith is and how to walk by faith on a consistent basis. You will also learn how to live out every miracle in the Bible (it is more simple than you think). Open your heart as we embark on a wonderful journey into the miraculous!

JESUS IS THE WORD

*For there **are three** that bear witness in heaven: the Father, the Word, and the Holy Spirit; and **these three are one** (1 John 5:7).*

There is a simple truth that many believers fail to realize; Jesus is the Word. To love Jesus is to love His Word. The Bible says that there are three who bear witness in heaven: the Father, the Word, and the Holy Spirit (see 1 John 5:7). This is what is commonly known as the Trinity. Notice that Jesus is referred to as the "Word." He is the *logos* made flesh. Once we realize "who" the Word is, then we can understand the importance of the Word of God when it comes to the life of faith. The Word is the key to unraveling the mystery of the miraculous.

This revelation of the Word literally transformed my life, and I know it will do the same for you. There are so many people in the body of Christ who reverence God's Word, but they have no power. There are others in the church who appreciate God's presence, but they have no regard for the Word. Both of these camps are missing out on a very important truth: the Spirit and the Word are one! We have to change the way we see things if we want to walk in God's supernatural power. In fact, the more you fall in love with the Word of God, the more you will recognize and appreciate the operation of the Spirit of God. The Word of God reveals the person of Jesus. This is the key to unleashing the power of faith in your life! Get ready to experience the fullness of God today.

FAITH DECLARATION

Father, I thank You that Your Word is the source of unlimited faith; Your Word is full of supernatural power. Through Your Word I am equipped to walk in the supernatural on a daily basis. I know that You created the visible universe with your spoken Word and that same creative power exists in the Word of God. Give me a hunger and desire to read, meditate on, and do your Word from this day forward. In the name of Jesus I declare. Amen!

2

FAITH FOUNDATIONS

*Now faith is the substance of things hoped for, the
evidence of things not seen* (HEBREWS 11:1).

ONE OF THE MOST IMPORTANT COMPONENTS TO WALKING IN THE
supernatural power of God is faith. It is through faith that the miraculous is released. What is faith? This is the question of the ages! You
might be surprised to know how misunderstood the subject of faith
really is. There have been countless movements in the body of Christ
that have expounded the teaching of faith, yet there still seems to be
somewhat of a disconnect among modern-day Christians. This question is born out of many years of personal experience both hearing
the Word and teaching the Word. If you and I are going to experience
the miraculous power of God, we need to have a solid foundation as
it relates to faith.

Again, what is faith? Hebrews 11:1 tells us that faith is the substance of things hoped for. What does this mean? The writer of
Hebrews used a very powerful word to express this truth. It is the
Greek word *pistis*. The simplest definition of this word is to have confidence or conviction of the truth of something. In short, our faith is

a *conviction*. Webster's dictionary defines *conviction* as a strong persuasion or belief. I believe it is much more than that (according to scripture), but this is a very good starting point. To have faith means to be fully persuaded. Persuaded of what? The truth! More specifically, you and I must be *fully* persuaded of the truth of God's Word.

The Bible doesn't stop there. In the latter part of Hebrews 11:1 it says, "the evidence of things not seen." Faith is not just confidence or conviction, but it is firm persuasion of what cannot be physically seen. In fact, it is the evidence of what we cannot see with our *natural* eyes. Now when the Bible says evidence, it is talking about the Greek word *elegchos,* which means proof. This is literally a legal term, which implies sufficient evidence in a courtroom. What the Word is literally saying is that in order to have faith, the jury of our heart (as it were) must be fully persuaded by the overwhelming evidence that God's Word presents.

So let's look again at what the Bible is saying and break it down a bit further: Faith (conviction) is the substance (support or substructure) of things hoped for (confidently expected and awaited with great anticipation) and the evidence (proof or legal evidence) of things not seen (invisible).

WHY SATAN HATES FAITH

We can already see from the aforementioned things that faith is an integral part of the Christian life. I would even go so far as to say that without it we cannot really live a Christian life at all. So why does the subject of faith seem so elusive to so many people? The Bible tells us in Hebrews 11:6, *"But without faith it is impossible to please Him* [God]...." Satan knows that if you and I learn to walk by faith in every area of our lives, we will ultimately be pleasing to God. Therefore, the enemy has strategically brought confusion in the area of faith. It seems that *faith* has become a taboo word.

Over the past 20 years, the church has embraced many dimensions of the New Testament paradigm, such as prophecy, apostolic ministry, the gifts of the Spirit, and revival culture; however, it seems that we have still fallen short in the area of faith. This subject has been smeared with abuse, misunderstanding, ignorance, and outright fear.

> *Once we learn to tap into this kind of faith, we are accessing the realm of the supernatural, and it is in this environment that we experience the miraculous.*

Why has this been the case? The most fearful thing that the devil could imagine is for the Church at large to learn to live a life of faith, more specifically—*unlimited faith*. By unlimited faith, I am referring to faith without limits imposed on it through religion, tradition, intellectualism, or the vain opinions of man. I am speaking of the faith that is willing to believe whatever the Word of God says without reservation or hesitation. Once we learn to tap into this kind of faith, we are accessing the realm of the supernatural, and it is in this environment that we experience the miraculous.

The Bible goes further to say, *"But without faith it is impossible to please Him, for he who comes to God must believe that He is, and that He is a rewarder of those who diligently seek Him..."* (Hebrews 11:6). To have faith in God is to first and foremost recognize who He is. This recognition is more than just a mere acknowledgment of God's power and sovereignty, it is an inner recognition of His very nature. This is why the scripture says that He is a rewarder of those who diligently seek Him. It is conveying to us the very nature of God. He is a good God! He is a rewarding God! As simple as this statement seems, I have met many Christians who do not really believe that God is good. Sure we sing about Him being good in a church setting, but that doesn't mean we really believe this truth.

If we know that He is good, then we would know that He is a rewarder of those who seek Him. This recognition would motivate our desire to seek Him even more. As they say in the country, "The proof is in the pudding." This simply means that if we believe something, we act on it. Faith is an action word (which we will discuss later). The more we are convinced of who God is, the more we will move toward Him with an expectation of being rewarded with the promises of His Word. Simply put, *faith is the inner recognition of and positive response to the Word of God.*

THE MAIN INGREDIENT

I love food. To tell you the truth I probably love food much more than I really should. I not only love eating food, but I also love to prepare it. When I was younger I would watch the food channels frequently. There would always be a highlight of some great recipe that was easy to put together. I discovered that the secret to any recipe or prepared dish is the main ingredient. An ingredient is defined as any of the foods or *substances* that are combined to make a particular dish or meal. In other words, the main ingredient is the essential component that causes something to be what it is.

Likewise, faith is the main ingredient in the Christian life. Faith is what causes everything that we know about God to come together and manifest supernatural living. Many Christians are struggling in their Christian walk because they are missing the main ingredient.

I can remember a time when I tried to make a particular dish as a young boy. The recipe called for white flour, but all I had at my disposal was corn meal; there is a difference! You can probably already imagine the outcome of this scenario. It turned out to be disastrous to say the least. Why? I was missing the main ingredient, and there is no substitute for the main ingredient. In the same manner, there is no substitute for faith. According to Hebrews 11:6, "But without faith it is impossible to please Him...." The word *impossible* in this passage literally means: *without strength, impotent, powerless, weakly, and disabled*. In other words, without faith (conviction of the truth of God's Word), our efforts to please God are impotent and powerless.

Many Christians believe that good intentions are enough to be pleasing to God. They believe that God should "know their heart," and this should be sufficient enough to experience His promises in their lives. This could not be further from the truth. The reality is that God is only moved by our faith, not by our feelings and emotions. In fact faith is so descriptive that you and I can always tell when we are walking by faith. The Bible says:

> *For indeed the gospel was preached to us as well as to them; but the word which they heard did not profit them, not being **mixed with faith** in those who heard it* (Hebrews 4:2).

This is one of my favorite passages of scripture because it literally changed the way I saw God forever. It tells us that the Word did not profit them. Who is "them" referring to? The writer of Hebrews is specifically talking about the Israelites who came out of Egypt after 430 years of slavery. These were God's chosen people. Here they were in the wilderness with remarkable promises given to them by God Himself, and yet they were not able to profit from those promises. The word *profit* in Hebrews 4:2 is the Greek word *opheleo* and it means to be advantageous. The promises of God were not useful or advantageous to them; they were literally impotent. Why? They were not mixed with faith.

Now the mixing referenced in this passage literally means to commingle or to combine several parts together. Sound familiar? It is similar to putting together a recipe. All of the components have to come together to make the dish what it was intended to be. The Israelites were missing the main component: faith. Even though they were God's chosen people who were endowed with God's covenant promises, their lack of faith prevented them from being able to enter the Promised Land at that time.

The writer of Hebrews is addressing this epistle to the church, which means the same thing applies to us. If you and I do not learn to consistently exercise faith in God's Word, His Word will become of no effect to us. Contrariwise, when you and I learn to consistently exercise unlimited faith, we will experience a world filled with God's unlimited miraculous power. Hallelujah! When you and I combine faith with the Word of God, it will become a divine recipe for supernatural living at its finest!

 Our faith is a firm foundation upon which the whole of our Christian experience is constructed.

A FIRM FOUNDATION

Growing up in Georgia, I had an opportunity to see many construction projects being undertaken. In fact, in the early nineties there was a boom of new construction in the neighborhood where I lived. One of the things that I noticed when I would observe new homes being constructed was the laying of the foundation. Unlike many cities that I have been to, most homes in Atlanta have basements. For this reason, builders have to take special care during the foundation phase of the home construction, because everything else depends on this part of the house. If the integrity of the foundation is compromised, then the entire home is compromised. A good home has a good foundation. To put it another way, a good home must have a firm foundation. A foundation is the base upon which everything else is built.

Our faith is a firm foundation upon which the whole of our Christian experience is constructed. Many people are attempting to have a healthy relationship with God without faith; this is not possible! It does not matter how beautiful a mansion is and how elaborate its interior; if the foundation is faulty, everyone in that home is in grave danger. Our faith is the basis for our interaction with our heavenly Father. I am not suggesting that faith is the only aspect to the Christian life, but it is foundational. This is why understanding how to walk by faith, according to the Word of God, is so vitally important.

You must remember that the life God intends for you is a life of power and victory. In Hebrews 11:1, when the Bible says that faith is the "substance," it is not just saying that faith is the main ingredient, but it is literally saying that faith is the "support" or "firm foundation" upon which the believer must stand in order to be pleasing to God. If you are a sincere Christian, pleasing God should be a priority. When laying a foundation there must be a substance that fills that foundation to make it sturdy. In the natural realm, the foundation is filled in with concrete. This causes the base to be hard enough and sturdy enough to support the weight of those who walk on it. In the Kingdom of God, the Word of God is the filler that gives strength and validity to our faith. Remember this: faith does not exist in a vacuum. We have to place our faith somewhere. The foundation of our faith is the integrity of God's Word. The reason why our faith can "support" us is because it is based in God's Word.

Don't Build Your House on Sand

As we mentioned before, faith is conviction of the truth of God's Word. We cannot simply base our faith on religious experiences. Jesus put it this way:

> *Therefore whoever hears these sayings of Mine, and does them, I will liken him to a wise man who built his house on the rock: and the rain descended, the floods came, and the winds blew and beat on that house; and it did not fall, for it was founded on the rock. But everyone who hears these sayings of Mine, and does not do them, will be like a foolish man who built his house on the sand: and the rain descended, the floods came, and the winds blew and beat on that house; and it fell. And great was its fall* (Matthew 7:24-27).

According to Jesus, those who are convinced of the truth of His Word and respond accordingly will weather any storm that comes their way because their "house" is built upon a rock. What is the rock in this passage? The Word of God! The Word of God is the concrete substance (or solid foundation) that acts as the basis for Kingdom living. Those who hear the Word and don't do it (because they don't believe it or respond positively to it) are like those who built their house on sand. You can probably imagine what would happen if a house built on sand was hit by a massive hurricane. It would undergo catastrophic damage to say the least! Sand is great for building sand castles, but horrible for building homes! This is what happens when you and I attempt to live our lives by emotions and not by faith in God's Word.

Beloved, faith is the key to supernatural living. Why? Because we serve an invisible supernatural God, and in order to please Him and enjoy the blessings He has graciously prepared for us, we must respond positively to what He says. Later in this book, you will learn practical insights that will thrust you into a deeper understanding of the supernatural, but in the meantime, I want to supply you with a basic understanding of faith. Interestingly enough, in the phrase "Whoever hears these sayings of Mine, and does them," the word *does* in this passage literally means to "construct." In other words, we are constructing our life of faith on the Word of God. Every time we act on God's Word in faith, our spiritual "house" becomes stronger and stronger, and the more resilient we become against the elements of the world. You and I have to make sure that our house is built upon the right foundation.

THE MEASURE OF FAITH

Contrary to popular belief, every born-again believer has faith. "What do you mean?" According to the Word of God, He has already dealt to every one of us "the" measure of faith. This is very important to understand. This understanding should be foundational to our theology. Theology is very important. The purpose of theology is not to win intellectual arguments, but to establish us in an understanding of the character and personality of God, especially in the midst of challenges. The Bible tells us in Romans 12:3:

> *For I say, through the grace given to me, to everyone who is among you, not to think of himself more highly than he ought to think, but to think soberly, as God has dealt to each one a* **measure of faith.**

What does the Bible mean when it says that God has dealt to every one of us "the measure" of faith? (A more accurate translation from the original Greek rather than "a measure.") The word *measure* is the Greek word *metron* and it literally means a measurement, quantity, or portion. God has distributed faith proportionally to every one of us. We have faith to believe Him right now because He gave it to us.

For years I believed that if I could just muster up enough faith then I would be able to trust God. This was absolute spiritual insanity. This thought process was even further enforced through religion and tradition. The truth was, I already had faith, and you do too. In fact, Jesus Himself is the author of our faith (see Hebrews 12:2). We must understand that God has given us all the necessary amount of faith that we need to believe and trust His Word. This amount of faith is a gift of God's grace, which He has deposited within us. In other words, you have the capacity to walk by faith and experience the miraculous right now!

We must understand that God has given us all the necessary amount of faith that we need to believe and trust His Word.

Then what is the issue? Why are there so many Christians who find it difficult to believe God? Why does the supernatural seem elusive to so many? It is very simple; they have not exercised their faith, and therefore it is weak. Faith is the muscular system of the spiritual realm. Like our physical muscles, it increases with use. You didn't do anything to earn your muscles, but you still need to use them. Muscles are developed! If you never exercise your physical muscles they will atrophy. Many believers are weak in faith, and as a result they are building their house on sand. They are unable to weather the storms of life. The Word of God says:

> *And Jesus said unto them, Because of your unbelief: for verily I say unto you, If ye have faith as a grain of mustard*

seed, ye shall say unto this mountain, Remove hence to yonder place; and it shall remove; and nothing shall be impossible unto you (Matthew 17:20 KJV).

There are two issues that Jesus addressed in this passage: unbelief and mustard seed faith. Jesus was responding to the disciples' inability to cast out a demon spirit. It is important to note that He previously gave them authority over all demon spirits. They had the power to do it. Why couldn't they do it? Jesus said that it was because of their unbelief. What does this mean? The word *unbelief* comes from the Greek word *apistia,* which means unfaithfulness or weakness of faith. Jesus attributed their inability to do what He gave them power to do to a weakness of faith, not an absence of faith. This rebuke was both counter cultural and counter religious, because everyone at that time believed that spiritual power was a result of religious piety and massive faith. Jesus dispelled these myths in His statement to the disciples.

The second thing He dealt with was the size of their faith. He said that "if they have faith as of a grain of mustard seed." Why is this so significant? Have you ever seen a mustard seed? A mustard seed is literally the size of a grain of sand. It is one of the smallest seeds on the planet. It is almost laughable for a person to attribute their faith to a seed that small. However, Jesus said that a little faith is all that is necessary to move a mountain and "nothing shall be impossible unto you." Wow! How can this be? Simple. The mustard seed is potent. It is packed with the power to manifest a great harvest. Faith is designed to bring manifestation.

UNBELIEF NEUTRALIZES FAITH

Again, what was the problem in the case of the disciples and so many in the body of Christ today? Even though they have faith, there is something else present inhibiting their faith from producing what it should. This thing is called unbelief. The issue was never the absence of faith, but the presence of unbelief. Unbelief neutralizes faith. If faith is a muscle, unbelief is a muscle relaxer (figuratively speaking). To put it another way, unbelief is a system of thinking contrary to the Word of God, which disables our ability to exercise the God-kind of faith. (We will talk about the God-kind of faith in a later chapter.)

Unbelief imposes limits on our faith that God never intended. These limitations are rooted in fear, misinformation, and deception. Satan knows that unlimited faith is devastating to his counterfeit kingdom; therefore he does everything in his power to neutralize it. How does he accomplish this task? Well, if faith is the conviction of the truth of God's Word, then unbelief is the conviction of a lie. When we are operating in unbelief we don't cease to believe, we simply believe something that is not true. The disciples were convinced that the demon they were facing was too great for them to deal with. This was a lie. They had all the authority they needed to deal with the devil.

 When we are operating in unbelief we don't cease to believe, we simply believe something that is not true.

I have even better news: you have all the authority that you need to deal with the enemy. You have the power at work in you to heal the sick, raise the dead, and cast out devils. You don't need more faith. You need to use what you have. What would happen if the Church at large suddenly realized that they already have all the faith they need to do the works of Jesus and greater according to John 14:12? We would literally experience an explosion of the power of God! The seed of faith within you possesses the latent power to manifest the supernatural. Why don't you put your faith to the test today!

FAITH DECLARATION

Father, in the name of Jesus I thank You for the truth and power of Your Word. I recognize that Your Word was the creative agent that brought the world into being. I delight in Your Word, Lord, and I meditate in its precepts day and night. Thank You for creating in me a hunger and a thirst for the Word of God. I don't want to go a single day without reading and studying the Word. Thank You that You have already given me the authority to address the powers of darkness operating in my life or the lives of those I love. Today I declare a release of Your miraculous power and presence in every area of my life in Jesus's name. Amen!

3

SEEING THE INVISIBLE

*By faith he forsook Egypt, not fearing the
wrath of the king: for he endured, as seeing
him who is invisible* (HEBREWS 11:27).

ONE OF THE FIRST TRUTHS THAT YOU AND I HAVE TO GRASP IN
order to operate in supernatural faith is that of seeing into the invisible
realm. That sounds like an oxymoron doesn't it? What does it mean
to see in the invisible realm? The Bible gives us several accounts of
great men and women of God who were able to experience supernatural moves of God by not being confined to the physical realm. They
were able to look beyond the natural to a world filled with unlimited
possibilities. You and I can do the same thing today!

One day I heard a story about a group of children who were
involved in a school science project. Their teacher wanted to open
their minds to the complex biological world around them. To prove
his point, he took his students to a pond and instructed them to
dip a glass jar into the pond and draw out a small amount of water.
Then he asked them if they saw all the magnificent creatures in the
water. Many of the children laughed and said, "There is nothing in

the water." So he took them to the lab and placed water from their jars under a microscope. As the students looked into the microscope, they were amazed by the movement and activity of living organisms within their glasses. Though they couldn't see these living organisms with their natural eyes, they were still very present and active.

The water from the pond is similar to the life of faith. The spiritual realm is alive and active, but many people are ignorant of this truth. In fact, we have been trained to become fixated upon the natural realm, as opposed to the spiritual realm. All of our lives we have been taught to rely upon what we can see, feel, taste, and smell. Once we come into the Kingdom of God we have to be retrained—we have to learn to see the invisible. The Bible says in Hebrews 11:27 that Moses actually forsook Egypt, not fearing the wrath of Pharaoh, because he endured as seeing Him who is invisible. The word *see* in this passage is the Greek verb *horaō* (Strong's G3708); this word literally means to see with the eyes or perceive. The question is: who did Moses see? He saw Him who is invisible. The word *invisible* is the Greek word *aoratos* (Strong's G517), which means unseen.

How was Moses able to see the invisible God? When most people think of invisible they think of nonexistence, but this is not what the Bible is speaking of at all. When was the last time you saw the wind? The reality is, the wind is invisible (for the most part). What we usually see are the effects of the wind. The point being, the wind is very real even though it cannot be seen with the natural eye.

SEEING THROUGH THE "EYES" OF FAITH

God has chosen in His sovereignty to cloak Himself in the invisible realm. Again, how then was Moses able to see or perceive God? Moses learned to see God through the eyes of faith. The Bible says "through faith." Our faith enables us to see in the spiritual realm.

Yes! Faith has eyes. Faith sees the power and nature of God and confidently awaits His manifestation. Just as the aforementioned children were able to see organisms, invisible to the naked eye by looking into a microscope, we are able to see into the realm of the Spirit by faith. Faith is the microscope of the spiritual realm. The reason why Moses was able to forsake Egypt (a land that seemed to offer much more wealth and pleasure than Canaan), was because he recognized that God was greater and more real than anything that the world's system could offer. Egypt represented the world system, which is governed by the five natural senses. The Bible says this:

> *Do not love the world or the things in the world. If anyone loves the world, the love of the Father is not in him. For all that is in the world—the lust of the flesh, the lust of the eyes, and the pride of life—is not of the Father but is of the world. And the world is passing away, and the lust of it; but he who does the will of God abides forever* (1 John 2:15-17).

 The first step to walking in the power of unlimited faith is to take our eyes off of the limitations of the natural and set our eyes on God's Word.

Everything in this world's system is designed to gratify our five natural senses. This can be categorized as the lust of the flesh and the lust of the eyes. This is exactly what Moses forsook. He rejected the offer to remain under the control of his flesh. Moses had a revelation of God by the Spirit. This revelation caused the eyes of his faith to open and allowed him to see into the invisible realm. He saw that God was much bigger and more powerful than Egypt would ever be. Simply put, he saw the promises of God's Word.

The first step to walking in the power of unlimited faith is to take our eyes off of the limitations of the natural and set our eyes on God's Word. The more you and I meditate upon the Word of God, the more we will see into the invisible realm. As a young believer, I can remember reading passages in the Bible and asking myself, "Is this real? Could these miraculous manifestations actually happen in my life?" The more I read about what the great men and women of God were able to accomplish through faith in God, the more I desired to see the supernatural in my own life.

The truth is that we were all wired for the supernatural. When God made man, He placed him in a supernatural environment and put the DNA of the supernatural within his very being. This is how we were created. Once man sinned, he became obsessed with the natural realm. Since the fall, we have secretly longed for that place. Satan knows this truth, and this is why he specializes in the counterfeit supernatural. This is why every movie and television show involves the New Age and occult, because Satan is attempting to draw people away from the authentic supernatural manifestation only experienced through faith in God's Word. The more we spend time with God as Moses did, the more we will experience His supernatural power in our lives. The key to living in the miraculous is developing the spiritual discipline of seeing the invisible through eyes of faith.

SEEING BEYOND THE NATURAL

There are countless people today who are bound, frustrated, and limited by the circumstances of their lives. Some are in a prison of debt and lack. Others are suffering the agony of a stressful marriage or a terminal illness. No matter where you may be in your life today, the key to experiencing breakthrough is the decision to look beyond your natural circumstances. This is the very nature of faith: to look beyond the current circumstance into God's promises for your life.

Everything about faith says the promises of God are more real than anything to the contrary. Faith reveals reality from God's perspective. Jesus understood this principle. This is how Jesus was able to walk on water. Faith had the power to change the Sea of Galilee to a sidewalk (see Matthew 14:25-27).

I can still remember a time when my wife and I had just started our church. We were so excited and expectant. After a while that expectation just turned into anxiety when the things we believed God to do did not seem to be happening. We were believing God for the finances to sustain our growing family after leaving our jobs and entering full-time ministry. We were also believing for God to open doors for the ministry that He called us to do. One day after a long and exhausting community outreach and evangelism event that didn't go as we had hoped, we were tired and discouraged. As was our custom, we came together and prayed.

Shortly after, my wife came to me and said, "Kynan, what do you see?" I proceeded to complain about our circumstances, then my wife interrupted me and asked again, "Kynan, what do you see?" Then it dawned on me that she was not talking about our natural circumstances; rather, she was talking about seeing the invisible. When I finally caught hold of what the Lord was saying through my wife, I immediately knew that it meant that if I could only see it, God was about to turn the situation around. Therefore, I began to open my eyes spiritually and declare the promises of God by faith concerning the people to whom we were ministering. The more we focused on seeing through the eyes of faith rather than what our current circumstances were saying, the more we became expectant and joyful. We realized that the current situation was only temporary.

All of a sudden, we saw a turnaround in our ministry and in our church. The things that I saw through the eyes of faith just a day earlier manifested in a glorious way. Why? Because His Word says so!

We took our eyes off of the limitations of our current circumstances and we began to see in the spirit. This does not come naturally to us; we must practice this on a daily basis. By faith, we look into the future and receive with confidence what God has promised us for our present. By faith, the promises of God are manifested in our lives. This is not a hit or miss gimmick or some religious formula; this is the spiritual key that God has given to His church to unlock the fullness of His Word in our lives—every day! Like Moses, you and I have to learn to look beyond what we see in the natural.

BELIEVING IS SEEING!

There is an old idiom used in the English language that says, "Seeing is believing!" In other words, people will come to a place of belief when they see proof or evidence. The truth is, when it comes to Kingdom living, believing is seeing! In the world, we are governed by what we can see. We believed that if we could see something then it must be real, and if we couldn't see something it must be unreal. The profound truth is that the invisible realm is of a deeper and truer reality than the natural realm.

 We have been given permission by God to see beyond this natural world into the invisible world by gazing through the eyes of faith.

Earlier we talked about the fact that God created the material world with invisible materiality. In other words, God's Word was the creative agency that brought the world as we know it into being. This is why Christians are not governed by the same philosophy that governs the world. We have been given permission by God to see beyond this natural world into the invisible world by gazing through the eyes of faith.

46

The Bible says in Hebrews 11:1 that, "faith is the substance of things hoped for, the *evidence* of things not seen." Faith in fact is the tangible evidence that substantiates that which we know to be true in the unseen realm. Even though we can't see it in the natural, we understand by faith that it is there.

For example, no one who is alive today walked the earth during the time of Christ, but we can declare with bold confidence that He is risen. How can you and I make such an amazing claim? We can do it by faith in the Word of God. Faith opens our eyes to the reality of the risen Savior. In the same manner, you and I no longer have to be confined by the natural realm in any area of our lives. It is not what we see that determines what we believe, it is what we believe that determines what we see. If you see yourself as a person with limits and hindrances who is unable to walk in victory, it is because you believe in a limited God. In the Gospel of John chapter 11, verses 39 and 40, the Bible records:

> *Jesus said, "Take away the stone." Martha, the sister of him who was dead, said to Him, "Lord, by this time there is a stench, for he has been dead four days." Jesus said to her, "Did I not say to you that if you would believe you would see the glory of God?"*

These words of Jesus are packed with revelation of the Kingdom of God as it relates to faith. Jesus was coming to raise Lazarus from the dead, and when He commanded the stone to be rolled away from Lazarus' tomb, He was met with objection from Martha. Why? Martha was concerned about the decomposing body of her brother being exposed. Embalming was not as sophisticated as it is today and there was going to be a potentially foul smell released from her brother's tomb. She believed in Jesus, but up to this point her belief was limited to Jesus the healer; now that Lazarus was dead, she did not believe that there was anything else Jesus could do. She believed in a limited God! Jesus responded to her by saying, "...if you would believe you would see the glory of God?" This is a supernatural key to experiencing the miraculous power of God. Believing!

If you and I will dare to believe, then we will see the Glory of God manifested in our lives. On the contrary, those who refuse to believe will not see the Glory of God. The word for "believe" in this passage is the Greek word *pisteuo* (Strong's G4100) and it means to be persuaded or to credit. Are you persuaded that God can do anything? Have you given God credit to His account that He is the miracle worker? The first thing that you and I have to do to enter the realm of miraculous living is to allow ourselves to be fully persuaded. The word *persuaded* simply means to be moved by argument. All of us have little lawyers inside our minds that argue against the reality of God's Word. These arguments try to talk us out of supernatural faith. You and I are persuaded when we make a conscious decision to put those internal lawyers to rest. The moment we believe God, the Glory of God is revealed. Believing is the doorway through which we see into the invisible realm. Believing is the divine entrance to supernatural encounters with God.

MOVING IN THE DIRECTION OF SIGHT

We were holding a healing meeting one night and there was a word of knowledge given concerning legs and knees being healed. All of a sudden the altar was filled with people who were having problems with their knees. As another minister and I were praying for the people, one by one they began to get healed instantaneously. However, there was one lady at the end of the line who was unable to walk without the assistance of a walker and whose legs were swollen stiff. I thought to myself, "God, how am I going to do this one?" I was looking at the situation from the natural perspective. Many in the church were hesitant to pray for this woman because of the severity of her condition. As I wrestled in my mind concerning what to do, I heard the Spirit of the Lord speak to me and He said, "You pray for her!" In my mind I thought, "What if she doesn't get healed, then I will really look bad." How many times have we done that? Yet, I kept feeling the tugging of the Holy Spirit, urging me to pray for this woman.

Finally, I surrendered to the Holy Spirit's leading. As I went to pray for her, I was met with several objections. She told me that I could not grab her arm because of her surgery. She said that she wasn't wearing the right kind of shoes, and so on! All of a sudden, bold faith arose in my spirit—the next thing I knew, I snatched the walker out of her hand and commanded her to walk. She looked in my eyes with amazement. I told her to no longer look down at her legs but to look at me, in the same way that Peter looked at Jesus while walking on the water (see Matthew 14:22-33). With each step forward, her faith became stronger and stronger until she went back to her seat, unassisted by a walker. To God be the glory! She was so excited that she began dancing around the church. She even brought another person to the altar (unassisted by her walker) to receive prayer.

The next day we received an email that this woman walked on her own for the first time in nine years. Praise God! What happened in this scenario? Both of us had to look beyond the natural realm in order to operate in unlimited faith. In my case, it was a matter of not regarding the severity of her condition but choosing to release my faith for her healing. In her case, it was a decision to believe that she could be healed of a condition that lasted nine years. In both cases, it was a matter of believing and seeing the Glory of God manifested.

What obstacle is standing in your way today? If you will dare to believe, you will see the Glory of God.

FAITH DECLARATION

Father, in the name of Jesus, I thank You for the truth and power of Your Word. By faith I open my eyes to the unseen realm, the realm of the Spirit, and I acknowledge that what exists in the unseen is of a truer and deeper reality than the natural realm. I am not moved by what I see in the natural, but the Word of God moves me. Thank You for the revelation of your Word in my life. Today, I train my spiritual eyes through prayer and meditation on the Word of God. I am fully persuaded that You can do anything. Today, I desire for every miracle in the Bible to become a reality in my life. In Jesus's name. Amen!

4

HOW FAITH COMES!

*So then faith comes by hearing, and hearing
by the word of God* (ROMANS 10:17).

How do we obtain faith? More importantly, where does faith come from? These are very important questions. Whenever I minister, I often get asked the question, "Can anybody do what you are talking about or is it just for ministers and really special people?" I always smile when I get asked this question, because the reality is that God wants all of His children to enjoy the blessings that He has prepared. He wants all of us to experience His supernatural power without limits.

Earlier, we mentioned that all it takes is mustard seed faith to move in the miraculous. The Bible tells us that God has dealt to every person *the measure* of faith. We also stated that our faith could be developed and strengthened with use. The question remains, how do we get the faith that we need to walk in God's supernatural power? Romans 10:17 tells us exactly where faith comes from, "Faith comes by hearing, and hearing by the word of God." What exactly does this mean? Simply put, confidence in the Word of God comes *from* the Word of God.

This is a twofold reality. On the one hand, we receive faith by the Spirit-filled proclamation of the Gospel of Jesus Christ. Paul says that it is the "power of God" to salvation for everyone who believes (see Romans 1:16). On the other hand, faith comes to us by the revelation of the Holy Spirit through the Word. In other words, the more you hear God's Word the more faith you receive.

The more we meditate upon the Word of God, the more the Holy Spirit speaks that Word into our spirit and the more revelation we receive. The more we receive revelation from the Word of God, the more faith we have. Notice that the Bible did not say that faith comes from hearing sermons. If this were the case, everyone who attended a church service would have great faith. In fact, the writer of Romans uses the Greek word *rhema* in reference to "the word." This is defined as the living voice or living Word. This means that the Bible has to become more than just a series of great stories; it must live inside us as the vital source of everything we hold true about God.

This is something that goes down deep into our inward man, which becomes a living conviction. Simply put, faith comes from the revelation of God's Word. This revelation comes to us through meditation. When I first became a believer, I didn't realize that I was practicing this biblical principle. Every day I would wake up and memorize a verse of scripture from the Bible and meditate on that scripture all day long. The more I did this, the more I received the boldness to live out what the scripture said. For example, if I read a scripture on evangelism, I would begin to confidently evangelize as the opportunity arose. Faith was coming and I didn't even know it. The more God revealed Himself to me through the Word, the more I found myself believing and trusting in Him. This is what the Bible means when it says that faith comes by hearing. This is the very reason why what we hear is so vitally important.

TAKE HEED TO WHAT YOU HEAR

As a pastor, I often wonder why it is so difficult for people to believe and trust God. We receive countless prayer requests about issues of sickness, disease, financial difficulties, and all sorts of other problems. Most of the people we hear from are so discouraged and despondent that they have practically given up on the Word of God. Then there are people who always fight with us when we tell them that they can live in victory and be blessed. It seems as if they don't want to hear the Word of God at all. Some of you may be in this place currently. Don't worry! This is not really your fault at all. What I have come to realize is that none of us can trust God beyond what we have heard about Him.

 The truth is that what we hear shapes our expectation, and our expectation in turn shapes our reality.

Imagine for a moment that you were taught your entire life that the earth was flat. What would happen if one day someone dared to challenge that view? They would be met with tremendous opposition. This is a spiritual principle. The truth is that what we hear shapes our expectation, and our expectation in turn shapes our reality. Have you ever been in an environment where people do not believe in miracles? Why don't they believe? They do not believe because they have heard or been taught the contrary. This is why the ministry that you sit under is vital to your spiritual development. Jesus put it this way:

> *Then He said to them, "Take heed what you hear. With the same measure you use, it will be measured to you; and to you who hear, more will be given"* (Mark 4:24).

This is a profound spiritual truth. Jesus declared that we should take heed to what we hear. Why did He say that, and what did He mean? The word used for "take heed" in this passage is the Greek word *blepo,* and it means to discern or to possess the power of seeing. Notice that Jesus exhorts His disciples to be discerning about what they hear. Why? He explains in the next part of this verse that "With the same measure you use, it will be measured to you...." Our Lord used agricultural verbiage to describe what takes place when we hear something. Whenever we receive something into our hearing it is like measuring grain into a container; whatever measure we take will determine the measure that we receive. In other words, whatever portion, measure, or extent we hear will yield an exponential return. This is the spiritual law of sowing and reaping.

The more we hear of a God with limits, the more limits we place on God. However, the more we hear about the God who can do the impossible, the more we will believe in a God who can do anything. All of this is determined by what we hear. This is the reason we must be very discerning as to what we are hearing on a consistent basis. If you are serious about walking in God's supernatural power, then you need to make some decisions today as to what you are going to allow into your ear gates. The Bible says, "So then faith comes by hearing, and hearing by the Word of God" (Romans 10:17). Notice that the passage does not say, "Faith comes by hearing the Word." This is a very important part of the equation that many Christians neglect. There have been times when I heard the Word day in and day out, and I still didn't believe God. Why? It is not enough to simply hear words coming out of a preacher's mouth, we have to *akouo* (the Greek word for hearing), which means to attend to or consider what we are hearing.

As we hear intentionally what the Word of God is saying it will in turn cause us to hear with spiritual ears inside us. This is the harvest that Jesus was referring to in Mark 4:24. This is the exponential manifestation of the Word that we hear. The Holy Spirit speaks the Word of God inside us, and when He does, faith comes. Simply put, if you want more of God's power in your life; change what you are hearing. The moment you start meditating on the Word of God with the intention of doing what you are meditating on, you will begin to see those things manifested in your life. So don't be frustrated if your life is not looking like the Bible says it should just yet; meditate on the Word of God and watch the power of God turn things around.

THE LIVING WORD

But Jesus answered him, saying, "It is written, 'Man shall not live by bread alone, but by every word of God'" (Luke 4:4).

One of my favorite Gospels is the Gospel of Luke. Luke's Gospel has the largest accounts of miracles and healing among the four. The other reason that I really enjoy this Gospel is because of the account found in Luke chapter 4. Here Jesus was tempted by the devil after fasting for forty days. While Jesus was hungry and thirsty, Satan showed up to tempt Him. In the third verse of Luke 4, Satan told Jesus, "If You are the Son of God, command this stone to become bread." What did Satan's comment signify? In essence, he was asking Jesus to take something that was inanimate and lifeless and transform it into something that can give nourishment and sustenance. This was a physical impossibility. Satan was mocking and taunting Jesus; he was challenging Him to prove His divinity.

The devil has been mocking this generation in the same way, challenging us to demonstrate our power and influence. To this challenge, Jesus responded in a very unexpected way. In the fourth verse of Luke 4, Jesus said, "It is written, 'Man shall not live by bread alone, but by every word of God.'" In other words, our lives do not simply consist of physical food, but we get our true sustenance and nourishment from God's Word. So many people today are simply feeding their physical man while their spiritual man is being severely neglected. This ought not be! Jesus said that we get our true life from the Word, not just rules and regulations recorded in the Bible, but the *rhema* or living Word.

The Word is the source of the miraculous, but it must be active inside of us in order for us to experience it.

In order for us to walk by faith and experience God's miraculous power, God's Word must be alive and active on the inside of us. In fact, the Kingdom of God should be experienced from the inside out, not from the outside in. By this I mean that we are not to measure our spiritual lives from our outward experiences, but the inner life is what determines what we manifest outwardly. People often say to me, "Pastor, I want to experience God's power in my life!" I ask them, "When is the last time you studied the Word of God?" Why do I ask this question? The Word is the source of the miraculous, but it must be active inside of us in order for us to experience it. I am not just talking about memorizing a few scriptures; I am talking about making the Word of God the very final authority in your life. Jesus was so full of God's Word that He could continue to stand firm amid great temptation. When God's Word truly becomes more real and powerful than anything else around us, then and only then will we begin to live a supernatural lifestyle as God intended.

A TESTIMONY OF FAITH

When our third child was very young, he had a severely herniated navel. We experienced this with our oldest daughter as well, and we were in a place where we didn't want to see it again in our children. One afternoon while my wife and I were in the house, we decided to do something about it. I was reminded of a scripture in Mark 11:23 which states, "For assuredly, I say to you, whoever says to this mountain, 'Be removed and be cast into the sea,' and does not doubt in his heart, but believes that those things he says will be done, he will have whatever he says." I immediately thought to myself that this should also apply to a herniated belly button. After all, the scripture does say, "he will have *whatever* he says." The more I meditated on the power of that scripture, the more audacious my faith became. Finally I declared that the mountain of hernia had to move according to Mark 11:23-24. We were amazed at what took place next. Literally, before our eyes, we saw the hernia shrink in a very short period of time. My wife yelled at me, "Kynan, look at his belly button!" Praise the Lord! I was amazed to see his belly button in a normal state.

How many other areas of our lives could use a manifestation of God's miraculous power? We have to take the limits off of what God can do. So many times we talk ourselves out of the miracle by rationalizing the Word of God. We say things like, "Well, I know God is not talking about a literal mountain!" or "Let's not go off the deep end now!" Why not? God's Word means exactly what it says. The moment I saw my son's belly button shrink, my faith was catapulted into a new dimension. I realized in that moment that if God could perform such a wonderful miracle on our behalf, then surely He could do anything. As you read this book and the testimonies it contains, I believe that your faith will move to a greater dimension as well.

MEDITATE ON THE WORD!

This Book of the Law shall not depart from your mouth, but you shall meditate in it day and night, that you may observe to do according to all that is written in it. For then you will make your way prosperous, and then you will have good success (Joshua 1:8).

One of the most powerful means of depositing the Word of God into your spirit and developing your faith is something called meditation. When I say meditation, I am not referring to Eastern meditation or retreating to a remote place and sitting on top of your head. When I mention meditation I am talking about an ancient Jewish tradition of muttering the promises of God to yourself. In fact, the Bible uses the word *hagah*. This is a Hebrew word that means to moan, growl, utter, mutter, or speak. The idea is that of speaking something over and over again to yourself.

Through this process, the Word of God begins to sink down into your subconsciousness and ultimately deep within your spirit man. We all have a spirit man who is gender neutral (see Galatians 3:28). The more we get the Word into our spirit, the more it produces a harvest of unlimited faith. The reality is that all of us meditate on a regular basis, whether we are conscious of it or not. God created us in His very image as speaking spiritual beings, so meditation comes natural to all of us. The real question is: on what are you meditating?

Almost every habit and behavior that we possess is a result of our consistent meditation. For example, people who are excessively negative tend to have a habit of pondering on and vocalizing negative thoughts, feelings, and emotions all day long. The Bible says, "For as he thinks in his heart, so is he" (Proverbs 23:7). What are you thinking and speaking to yourself on a regular basis? Are you declaring the

Word of God, or are you filling your mind and mouth with doubt and unbelief?

The Bible commands us in Joshua 1:8 that, "This Book of the Law *shall not depart from your mouth....*" What does this mean? First of all, when the Bible refers to the Law it is not simply referring to the Ten Commandments (although it is making specific reference to them in this passage), but the Hebrews understood the Law to be the *express* Word of God. This is the Hebrew word *torah* or *towrah* (הרי Strong's H3384). It was God's sovereign instruction directly from heaven. Simply put, Joshua was commanded by God to meditate upon His Word day in and day out. We are not only commanded to meditate on the Word of God day and night, but we are instructed to meditate on the Word of God with the intent to do what it says. Hallelujah!

The Bible is absolutely true, and everything God says therein will come to pass in your life if you will simply become diligent in meditating on the Word every day and silencing every other voice around you.

We are not to simply quote a bunch of scriptures aimlessly, we are to observe them with a sense of intentionality and purpose; our purpose is to see the Word manifested in our lives practically. The scripture does not just conclude there, but there is a powerful promise attached to this instruction. When we meditate on the Word of God with the intent to do what is written therein, the Bible says that we will make our way prosperous and have good success. In other words, we will advance, succeed, and become profitable in our spiritual and physical lives. I don't know about you, but I like the sound of becoming profitable in the things of God.

THE WORD OF GOD WORKS!

Simply put, the Word of God will work for you! To be quite honest, there was a time in my life when the Word of God didn't seem to work for me. I limited God to my experiences and the experiences of others. When I grabbed hold of this passage of scripture, all of that seemed to change. I realized that I was the problem, not the Bible. The Bible is absolutely true, and everything God says therein will come to pass in your life if you will simply become diligent in meditating on the Word every day and silencing every other voice around you.

The more I did this, the more my faith grew. All of a sudden I was able to believe God for the impossible and experience the miraculous. The more you mutter the Word of God to yourself with the mindset of doing what you are muttering, the stronger your faith will become and miracles will be your new normal. I want you to make this faith confession out loud:

> *Father, in the name of Jesus, I thank You for who You are and all that You have done. Right now in the name of Jesus I decree and declare that I have great **faith**. In accordance with Mark 11:22-23, I have the God-kind of faith, and every mountain in my life and in the lives of those around me must obey my voice. I open my mouth right now and I say that doubt and unbelief must go from me. I am a believer of the Word of God. Every word in the Bible is the truth and I believe it. The Word of God is the final authority in my life. I am not moved by what I see; I am only moved by the Word of God. I walk by faith in the Word of God and not by sight. I am not controlled by my emotions, the emotions of others, or my environment; I am completely dominated by God's Word. Romans 10:17*

declares that faith comes by hearing and hearing by the Word of God. I am a hearer of Your Word and as a result I have great faith. Faith is the revelation of God's Word in action; therefore I am a doer of Your Word. Nothing is impossible to me because I am a believer of Your Word. In Jesus's name. Amen!

5

THE LAW OF CONFESSION

That if thou shalt confess with thy mouth the Lord Jesus,
and shalt believe in thine heart that God hath raised him
from the dead, thou shalt be saved. For with the heart
man believeth unto righteousness; and with the mouth
confession is made unto salvation (ROMANS 10:9-10 KJV).

EARLIER IN THE BOOK, WE DISCUSSED THE PROFOUND POWER OF the Word of God. Have you ever wondered, out of all the means available in God's infinite wisdom, why He chose to create the world with the spoken Word? This may be one of the most profound spiritual revelations in the Bible. When God spoke to the darkness and said, "Let there be light," He was not just establishing the physical world, He was setting a spiritual precedent; He was establishing a spiritual law. It is clear through the Bible that words shape the world around us. I discovered early in my life that words have the power to hurt or heal.

The Bible says that death and life are in the power of the tongue (see Proverbs 18:21). In fact, several years ago, there was research done in the field of what is known as cymatics. This is essentially the study of how the vibration of sound (in the form of words) has the power to move matter. Ultimately, everything in the created world was spoken into being and therefore responds to the spoken word. I will spare you all the cryptic details, but the point is that science is just beginning to catch up with the Word of God.

The Bible says in Romans 10:9 that if we will confess with our mouth the Lord Jesus and believe in our heart that God has raised Him from the dead that we will be saved. There are two very powerful elements to this passage of scripture that we cannot afford to ignore. The first is the element of confession (or the act of confessing). This is the Greek word *homologeo,* and it means to say the same thing as another or to say what has been said. Confession is an act of volition that involves coming into verbal agreement with someone or something. Our first encounter with the lordship of Jesus Christ is essentially a confession. We come into divine agreement with what He says about us and what He says about Himself.

SAY WHAT GOD SAYS!

The second element is that of whom we are to confess. The Bible says that we are to confess with our mouth that Jesus is Lord (see Romans 10:9). What does it mean to confess the lordship of Jesus? John 1:1 tells us that *"In the beginning was the Word, and the Word was with God, and the Word was God."* In other words, Jesus Christ is the Word of God personified (or made flesh). To confess Him as Lord essentially means to admit with your mouth that His Word (both written and revealed by the Holy Spirit) is the final authority in your life. The Bible doesn't stop there. In Romans 10:10 it states, "For with the heart one believes unto righteousness, and with the mouth confession is made unto salvation." This is known as the *Law of Confession.* By Law of Confession, I am not referring to some secular exercise in positive thinking (apart from God). I am specifically referring to the biblical practice of saying what God says.

Every miraculous manifestation in our lives, including salvation, begins with the words that we speak. In fact, almost everything in your life is the result of words spoken and words believed. Many years ago, I was sitting in my living room and I saw a famous television preacher on my television set by the name of John Osteen, who preached a very simple message. At the end of his message, he gave an altar call for salvation. He described this wonderful place called heaven. I can remember looking at my mother and asking her if I could say the prayer of salvation. She said, "Yes!" I was about nine years old at the time. This was my first encounter with confessing the Lord Jesus. How could something so simple change my life? How could something so seemingly insignificant to the world be the catalyst for the greatest miracle known to mankind (salvation)? Eternal salvation was introduced to me through the preaching of the gospel, and through words coming out of my own mouth. This is not just a positive thinking exercise that makes us feel happy; this is a spiritual law that must be respected and observed by all believers, especially those who are interested in walking in the supernatural.

Every miraculous manifestation in our lives, including salvation, begins with the words that we speak.

LOGOS VS. RHEMA

In the book of Romans chapter 10, Paul explains to the church in Rome what faith is all about. In this epistle, Apostle Paul states that the Israelites of his day possessed zeal for God, but not according to knowledge. They were ignorant of God's righteousness and going about to establish their own righteousness. Why were the Israelites attempting to do this? Simply put, they did not have a spiritual understanding of the Law. We know from scripture that the Law was absolutely perfect, but it alone did not have the capacity to bring salvation. Jesus, during His earthly ministry, exposed a similar flaw during His open rebuke of the Pharisees: "You *search the Scriptures,* for in them you think you have eternal life; and these are they which testify of Me" (see John 5:39). What was Jesus saying? He was explaining to the Pharisees that just because they knew what the scriptures said did not mean that they possessed eternal life. They understood religious jargon and philosophy, but this did not translate into a deeper understanding and spiritual freedom. The Pharisees were masters of the written Word of God. In fact, most of them could recite the Torah from memory. They understood the principles and the doctrines of the Bible, but they did not possess the supernatural fruit of such knowledge. If they really had a spiritual understanding of the Torah (the way God intended), they would have been able to clearly recognize the Messiah. This is what I call the difference between the *logos* and the *rhema* Word of God.

Earlier, we discussed that the Word of God was present in the beginning. In the Gospel of John, the Bible uses the Greek word *logos* to express this truth. When we use the word *logos* we are referring to "a thought or principle." In other words, the *logos* deals with precepts and principles that God declares to us as truth in His Word. This is the written Word of God. The Pharisees and Sadducees were masters of the written Word of God, but they were completely ignorant of the *rhema*, or living Word of God. If you and I are going to live in the miraculous consistently, it is not enough for us to possess the *logos*—we must also possess the *rhema*. We must know the written and the living Word. How do we possess the *rhema* of God? The Bible tells us in Romans 10:8, "But what does it say? *"The word is near you, in your mouth and in your heart* (that is, the word of faith which we preach)." Paul is quoting from the book of Deuteronomy chapter 30 verses 12 through 14.

> *It is not in heaven, that you should say, "Who will ascend into heaven for us and bring it to us, that we may hear it and do it?" Nor is it beyond the sea, that you should say, "Who will go over the sea for us and bring it to us, that we may hear it and do it?" But the word is very near you, in your mouth and in your heart, that you may do it.*

Essentially, the Bible says that the Word of God that brings salvation (deliverance, healing, restoration, manifestation, and change) is the Word that is in our mouths. This "word" is not in some far off or mystical place, it is in our mouths. Our mouth is the incubator that facilitates the transformation of the Word from *logos* to *rhema*. This is the Word that brings supernatural manifestation in our lives. Once the Word of God goes deep down into your spirit and you release that Word out of your mouth (with corresponding action), it is literally pregnant with the miracle working power of God. This becomes more than a principle or idea, it becomes the living Word. The Word of God must be alive and active on the inside of us. We must speak the Word in faith on a consistent basis for it to produce the results that God promises.

Let me be clear: speaking or confessing alone is not faith, but the revealed Word of God manifests faith. This is a very important spiritual truth of which many people are ignorant. The Bible says, "And you shall know the truth, and the truth shall make you free" (John 8:32). The knowing referenced in this passage is not a simple head knowledge or mental assent. This knowing is a deep intimacy. This is the Greek word *ginosko* (Strong's G1097), which is a transliteration of the Jewish idiomatic word that means to engage in intercourse.

It is the intimacy that a husband and wife experience. This intimacy always produces fruit. Once we become intimately acquainted with the living *(rhema)* Word of God, it will bring manifestation into our lives.

CONFESSION BRINGS POSSESSION

I cannot stress enough the importance of confessing the Word of God as it relates to activating God's miraculous power in your life. The Bible says in Hebrews 4:12, "For the word of God is living and powerful, and sharper than any two-edged sword, piercing even to the division of soul and spirit, and of joints and marrow, and is a discerner of the thoughts and intents of the heart." The Word of God is alive and full of power! We are not just talking about chapters and verses, we are talking about the Omnipotent Power who created the very universe. We are talking about the Spirit of the Word. When was the last time you viewed the Word of God from that perspective? Most people don't think about the Word that way, and this is why most people never experience the miracles that they read about in the Bible.

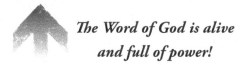

The Word of God is alive and full of power!

We found out earlier that the Word of God is the basis for our faith in God. In the same way, confession is the spiritual mechanism of faith that releases the latent power of the Word. This *spiritual* mechanism is essential to the Christian life. In fact, real faith must confess God's Word in order to possess God's Word. In the book of Romans, chapter 10, the Bible says:

For with the heart one believes unto righteousness, and with the mouth confession is made unto salvation (Romans 10:10).

We said earlier that to believe something means to accept it as true. In other words, when you accept something as true, you respond to it accordingly. For example, if you were told by the weather forecaster that there was a 100 percent chance of rain, yet you chose to leave the house without an umbrella, it would be safe to say that you probably did not believe the forecaster, right? Why? Belief requires action. Belief takes place in our heart (the soul or mind). The Bible says that with the "heart" man believes unto righteousness, and with the "mouth" confession is made unto salvation. In other words, it is not enough to believe in your heart; you must also confess with your mouth. Why is this so important? Confession is a spiritual law that governs all of creation.

Again, God Himself spoke the world into being; He did not simply think or imagine the world into being. There must be a connection between the Word believed and the Word spoken. So many Christians are falling short in their experience with God because they have not learned the spiritual discipline of confessing God's Word. You must say something! You must speak to those mountains in your life! Don't sit back and be quiet.

The Bible says: *"And since we have the same spirit of faith, according to what is written, 'I believed and therefore I spoke,' we also believe and therefore speak"* (2 Corinthians 4:13). Simply put, believing requires speaking. *Confession is the corresponding action of faith.* The evidence that we really believe is that we say what we believe out of our mouths, consistently. Someone might say, "Oh, that is just name it and claim it!" Don't let the devil deceive you. This is not about some positive thinking exercise (though it is very important to have a positive mental attitude), this is about standing on the integrity of God's Word in order to see that Word manifested in your life.

POSSESSED BY THE WORD

I have ministered to countless people who have refused to confess the Word, and they are suffering as a result of it. This is not the will of God. We must possess the promises of God that we read in the Bible. What do I mean by possessing the promises? I mean that we must take ownership over the promises of God. We must believe without equivocation that they belong to us. We must know beyond the shadow of doubt that the Word is absolute truth. This is not the philosophy of man, but the Word of the Living God. However, I want to take it a step further. Once we learn to confess the Word of God (say what God says), then that Word which we confess will possess us. We will become completely filled and dominated by the Word and the power contained therein. Just like possession takes place in a demonic sense, the person being possessed is controlled by the entity to the point of manifesting the attributes of that spirit in thought, speech, and action. In the same way, God wants to possess us!

Unlike demons, God wants us to offer ourselves to Him willingly. We do this through the act of confessing (among other things). Whatever you confess will ultimately possess you. Some people are constantly speaking fear-filled words. They complain, murmur, worry, and pronounce death over themselves and others. As a result, they are completely dominated by doubt, fear, guilt, anxiety, and calamity. Contrariwise, if we will learn to confess the Word of God, we will be filled with supernatural power and ultimately manifest that power in our thoughts, speech, and actions.

Today you need to make the decision to allow the Word of God to possess your mind, will, and emotions. In fact, if you want to live in the realm of the supernatural, it will begin with changing the words coming out of your own mouth. Take a serious inventory of your words. What are you speaking on a consistent basis? This will help you to understand where you are spiritually and what changes you need to make.

RELEASE THE SUPERNATURAL

We can never underestimate the power of speaking faith-filled words constantly. I for one have seen the demonstration of this divine principle in my personal life. I can remember a time when I was being afflicted in my physical body with sickness and disease. I was so frustrated. Here I was seeing countless people being healed and delivered, yet the enemy was attacking my physical body. Like most people, I prayed. I asked God to heal me. It seemed like the more I prayed for healing, the worse the symptoms became. I would experience severe numbness in my face, arms, and feet. The devil began to speak to my mind and tell me that I had a very severe chronic condition. "Lord, heal me!" I cried.

 You must understand that you already have the supernatural power of God resident within you. You have the life-giving Word in your heart.

Then one day as I was praying, I heard the still small voice of the Holy Spirit. He said to me, "Son, why are you asking Me to do what I have already done?" I was puzzled by this question. Then the Holy Spirit said to me, "You were already healed two thousand years ago. Speak to your body and command it to align with My Word." I never looked at things from that vantage point before. I stopped asking God to heal me, and I started confessing that I was already healed. There was absolutely no change at first; at least that is what

71

I thought. All of a sudden, each of the symptoms began to abate. As I continued to confess healing and wholeness over my body, every symptom left and did not come back! Hallelujah to the Lamb of God! What took place in this situation? I had to release the power of God by speaking the *rhema* Word of God.

You must understand that you already have the supernatural power of God resident within you. You have the life-giving Word in your heart. In order to experience the miraculous, you have to release that power. We release the supernatural through confessing the Word of God on a regular basis. You already possess the Spirit of Faith according to 2 Corinthians 4:13. So speak life over yourself!

INTERNALIZE THE WORD

In the Gospel of Matthew chapter 17, Jesus addressed His disciples very sternly in response to their inability to deliver a young boy from demonic oppression. They prayed for this young man to no avail. After Jesus rebuked them, the disciples came to Him privately and asked, "Why couldn't we cast him out?" To this question, Jesus responded:

> *Because of your unbelief; for assuredly, I say to you, if you have faith as a mustard seed, you will say to this mountain, 'Move from here to there,' and it will move; and nothing will be impossible for you* (Matthew 17:20).

Notice that Jesus attributes their spiritual ineffectiveness to unbelief. He never once addressed their piety or their works. All that was necessary to bring deliverance to that young boy was genuine "mustard seed" faith. This passage makes religious people cringe. We have been taught to buy in to formulas and strategies. There are so many messages on five steps to deliverance and seven steps to breakthrough, et cetera. However, Jesus calls into question their faith, and their faith alone.

There is an even more powerful key to manifesting the supernatural, which we see illustrated in the latter part of this verse. Jesus said, "Because of your unbelief; for assuredly, I say to you, if you have faith as a mustard seed, you will say to this mountain, 'Move from here to there,' and it *will* move; and *nothing will be impossible for you.*" What did Jesus mean when He said "nothing will be impossible for you"? In the original Greek, this statement says, "No *Rhema* shall be void of power." Now this changes things a bit, doesn't it? Everyone likes to believe that they have great faith, but as they say in the country, "The proof is in the pudding!" In other words, faith always brings manifestation.

It is not enough to go to church and memorize a few Bible verses. The Word of God must become *rhema* inside you. Once the Word becomes *rhema*, we will speak it forth, and it will not be void of God's miracle working power. If the disciples really believed God, if they really internalized the words of Jesus, they would have spoken to the young man with authority and power, and he would have experienced true deliverance.

We mentioned earlier that *rhema* means living voice, utterance, or spoken word (Strong's G4487). If you want to see the promises of God come alive, you have to start confessing them in faith and expectation (we will talk more about the Law of Expectation in a later chapter). We are not just talking about mental assent; we are talking about deep conviction and trust in God. The Bible says, "So shall My word be that goes forth from My mouth; it shall not return to Me void, but it shall accomplish what I please, and it shall prosper in the thing for which I sent it" (Isaiah 55:11). God's Word, is full of life and power. The moment God speaks His Word; it goes to work on His behalf. It is no different with us. Remember, we are not speaking our own words; we are speaking the Word of God. This is what confession *(homologeo)* is all about; we are saying what God has already said.

Declare the Word of God right now! The moment you speak the Word in faith and confidence, it will go to work on your behalf. It will never return void.

FAITH DECLARATION

Father, in the name of Jesus, I thank You for all that You have done in my life. I know that Your Word will never return void; therefore I boldly confess Your Word, knowing that it will surely come to pass in my life. Today I affirm that I am a believer and not a doubter. Your Word will never be void of miracle working power, but it will accomplish what You have sent it to do. I speak Your Word in faith now! I take authority over all fear, anxiety, and doubt, and I declare that I possess deep conviction of the truth of Your Word. I internalize every promise in the scriptures concerning my future and the future of my loved ones. I will live and not die and declare the works of the Lord. In the name of Jesus! Amen!

6

FAITH FOR MIRACLES

Therefore He who supplies the Spirit to you and works miracles among you, does He do it by the works of the law, or by the hearing of faith?—just as Abraham "believed God, and it was accounted to him for righteousness" (Galatians 3:5-6).

As you have already seen, faith is a profound spiritual reality for the believer. It is the basis from which all manifestation in the Kingdom of God flows. The Spirit-filled life of faith is the divine inheritance of every single believer in Jesus. We are not just called to follow the teachings of Jesus or to emulate His character, we are called by God to manifest the Kingdom of God and to display its power. How do we accomplish this? We do not accomplish this through religion, tradition, or legalism; we are only able to accomplish this through walking by faith. Simply put, we are called to live in the miraculous daily.

I was asked once, "If miracles become common place, are they still miracles?" The answer to this question is, "YES!" Maybe I should define miracles. When we use the term miracle, we are referring to a manifestation of God that interrupts, suspends, or violates the very laws of nature. We are talking about divine intervention. This intervention circumvents, or overrides, natural processes. For example, creative miracles: a person receiving a brand-new heart, food multiplying, and the like.

I was just a teenager when I witnessed my first miracle. We were in a regular Bible study when a lady came to the altar for prayer. One of her legs was significantly shorter than the other. The man of God sat her down, grabbed her legs, and commanded them to grow. In my mind I thought, "This is ridiculous!" To my surprise, the leg grew right before my eyes. Hallelujah! At the time, I did not know that this sort of manifestation should be normal in the church. Unfortunately, many of you reading this still don't know that this should be normal. Why? We have replaced the supernatural with philosophy and pseudo-intellectualism, often masked as theology. I am not saying that we should dismiss theology. I am saying that when we get our theology right, it will facilitate the supernatural.

YOU ALREADY HAVE MIRACLE FAITH

One of my favorite epistles in the Bible is Apostle Paul's epistle to the Galatian church. This epistle was probably written around AD 60. During this time, there was a severe problem in the church in Galatia. There were people known as Judaizers (Jewish believers in the church, zealous for the law), who were subverting the faith of Gentile believers through the practice of legalism. They were convincing misinformed Gentile believers that they needed to be circumcised and practice the Laws of Moses in order to be saved. Paul confronts this false teaching very aggressively and goes as far as to call this "another gospel."

In the third chapter of Galatians, Paul asked the church a profound question: "O foolish Galatians! Who has bewitched you that you should not obey the truth, before whose eyes Jesus Christ was clearly portrayed among you as crucified?" (Galatians 3:1). The word "bewitched" literally means to cast a spell on someone. Paul goes further to say, "This only I want to learn from you: Did you receive the Spirit by the works of the law, or by the hearing of faith?" (Galatians 3:2). Why does he pose this question? The implication is that their salvation came through faith and not religious works. When we come to God by faith, He accepts our faith as the means of bringing us into His Kingdom. God doesn't ask us to recite the Torah or become circumcised before we can be saved. He simply asks us to believe that Christ's sacrifice was the sufficient payment for our sins.

The same faith that saves from sin is the same faith that manifests the miraculous power of God.

When we repent of our sins and believe the Gospel we are saved. Why is this so important? The same faith for salvation is the same faith for miracles! In Galatians 3:5, Paul says, "He who supplies the Spirit to you and works miracles among you, does He do it by the works of the law, or by the hearing of faith?" This is known as a rhetorical question. In other words, he is telling us that the working of miracles is a matter of faith. The same faith that saves from sin is the same faith that manifests the miraculous power of God. The problem is that many people are ignorant of this truth. Frankly, they do not even regard their salvation as a miracle.

Beloved, to transform a sinner into a saint is nothing short of miraculous! Therefore, if the greatest miracle of all was simply a matter of taking God at His Word, then every other display of the miraculous is no different. Unfortunately, many people have been "bewitched" into believing that they don't have "enough faith" or that they need to come up with some religious formula to walk in the miraculous. This is simply not true! God has given all of His children the ingredients they need to experience the life He intends, which is a supernatural life!

THE HEARING OF FAITH

If you and I are going to experience the miraculous power of God, we are going to have to develop our spiritual sense of hearing. This is what Paul calls *"the hearing of faith."* The word *hearing* is the Greek word *akoe* (Strong's G189) and it literally means "sense of hearing." Interestingly, this is the same word found in Romans 10:17 where it says, "So then faith *comes* by hearing, and hearing by the word of God." We see then that hearing is an important part of the life of faith. In the case of salvation, we heard the gospel and believed, and as a result we experienced the miracle of salvation. Salvation is a matter of hearing. Likewise, miracles are a matter of what you hear.

We live in an age of sound. There are all kinds of sounds around us. Daily we are bombarded with thoughts, suggestions, and influences. The news channels tell us how we ought to feel and how we ought to think. The enemy knows that what we hear has a profound effect on what we believe, and what we believe determines what we receive. Therefore, he works overtime to saturate our minds with thoughts of doubt, unbelief, and despair. Earlier, I mentioned the importance of seeing the invisible, but I want to also reemphasize the importance of hearing. This spiritual sense of hearing Paul refers to must be developed through the disciplines of daily Bible study and intimacy with the Holy Spirit.

Did you know that every doubt in your mind was seeded by something you heard? For example, someone told you that the economy is going to get bad, and this is why you hold that belief. A doctor told you that a certain sickness "runs in your family," and this is why you are anxious about your future. In the same manner, unlimited faith is produced by what you hear. We must realize that we serve a God who can do anything. That is right, I said anything! Can you believe that? This realization only comes from us spending time digesting the Word of God. As I have said before, the more you read about the miracles of the Bible, the more you will desire to see those miracles, and the more your faith will rise, and ultimately you will experience those very miracles.

MIRACLES IN PRACTICE

When I first became a believer, I was so zealous for the things of God. I literally read my Bible for hours on end. The more I read, the more I was provoked to a godly jealousy. I thought to myself, "Why can't I experience this?" I was so desirous to see the Bible come alive that I looked for every opportunity to demonstrate the power of God.

One day as a teenager in high school, I noticed that something was wrong with one of my classmates. She wore black every day and she never spoke to anyone. I asked her if she knew Jesus. She said, "No." I also discerned that there were malevolent forces at work inside her. I didn't know many scriptures, but from what I read I led her in a prayer of deliverance and salvation. I took authority over the spirit of suicide and death, and immediately she was set free by the power of God. Wow! The more I heard the Holy Spirit speak to me through the Word, the more my faith would rise to the occasion.

On another (more recent) occasion, a man contacted our ministry for prayer. He purchased one of our books on healing and listened to our teachings. Prior to this time, he never saw a single sick person healed or a single miracle. One day after reading my book and meditating on the scriptures, he decided to put what he read into practice. So he went to the local pharmacy and began to pray for people going in and out of the pharmacy. One such person was an elderly man suffering from blindness as a result of cataracts. He laid hands on and prayed for this person, and instantly the man was able to see clearly. Hallelujah! Faith comes by hearing and hearing by the Word of God. This gentleman exercised his sense of spiritual hearing, and as a result of acting on what he heard he experienced the miraculous. The same will stand true for you as you hear the voice of the Holy Spirit right now!

Don't Harden Your Heart

Today, if you will hear His voice, do not harden your hearts as in the rebellion (Hebrews 3:15).

The simple truth is that you and I have a profound choice before us. Are we going to listen to the voice of the Spirit of God or are we going to listen to the voice of fear and doubt? The reason why I was able to walk in the power of God was due to my willingness to yield to the Holy Spirit. Many faith teachers don't talk much about the Holy Spirit, but He is essential to the life of faith, particularly "unlimited faith." In fact, during my studies of the great men and women of faith in the Bible and the modern church, I noticed one common theme: intimacy with the Holy Spirit. We know that faith comes by hearing, but the Bible doesn't stop there. If we continue to read Romans 10:17, we will see that hearing comes by the Word of God.

 The key to faith and miracles is hearing; therefore it would only stand to reason that you and I should invest significant time acclimating ourselves to God's voice.

We said earlier that this hearing is a spiritual hearing *(akoe)* produced by the Holy Spirit. When you and I meditate on the Word, that Word goes deep into the recesses of our being as a seed. The

Holy Spirit breathes life on that seed and it produces a supernatural harvest inside us. As a result of this divine process, you and I receive the faith necessary to believe God at the level He reveals Himself. This seems simple enough, doesn't it? What then is the problem? The problem that many people have is that they have not developed sensitivity to the Holy Spirit. The key to faith and miracles is hearing; therefore it would only stand to reason that you and I should invest significant time acclimating ourselves to God's voice. However, many people have become hardened to the voice of the Lord. This hardness is a result of a departure from delighting themselves in the Word of God and being obedient to His instruction. The responsibility of the Holy Spirit is to testify of the risen Christ and lead the believer into all truth.

INTIMACY WITH THE HOLY SPIRIT

During this technological age, there are many distractions. Many things and people are vying for our time, attention, and devotion. Whoever you choose to give ear to will become the one who governs your life, whether entertainment or the Holy Ghost. Will you yield to the Spirit or to your flesh? The word for "hardness" comes from the Greek word *sklērynō*, which means (in a figurative sense) to render obstinate or stubborn. Our reality is shaped by what comes in and out of our ear gates and eye gates. Do you dedicate time each day to listening to the Holy Spirit? Are you obedient to Him when He speaks? This is critical!

If we don't make the decision to spend quality time with the Holy Spirit and saturate our mind with the Word with the intention of obeying, we run the serious risk of becoming hard, stubborn, and obstinate; ultimately we will begin to be consumed by doubt, skepticism, and unbelief. This is essentially what it means to harden your heart. How are you going to see a supernatural healing if you don't listen to the Holy Spirit when He tells you to pray for a particular person? How are you going to experience supernatural provision if you are not receptive to detailed instructions from the Spirit on what to do and where to go? This is a key to releasing the power of unlimited faith in your life. Start today by spending time in the Word of God and allowing God to speak to you by His Spirit.

So many people in the church are suffering from hardened hearts. They have convinced themselves that the natural realm is more real than the spiritual realm. Many have even believed the lie that miracles don't happen anymore; this couldn't be further from the truth. You may be in a place of doubt and unbelief due to the hardness of your heart; you don't have to stay that way. Ask the Lord to soften your heart. Ask Him to restore you to a place of childlike faith and obedience.

FAITH VS. WORKS

For many years I thought that I had to be a great Christian figure and a really dynamic person to walk in signs, wonders, and miracles. The truth is, most of the prominent figures in the Bible and in the past 250 years of modern church history have been average people who simply believed God. Experiencing God's power is not a matter of human effort or works of the law, it is a matter of simple, audacious faith. Religion and tradition have placed a glass ceiling on the church. We come up with excuses and intellectual arguments as to why we are not seeing the power of God demonstrated today that we saw in the first century church. Some say that the gifts are no longer in operation. Others blame geography, politics, denominationalism, and sin for why we are not flowing in the supernatural. Many people assume that miracles only happen in third world nations.

I don't believe it has anything to do with those things at all. I believe the reason we are not seeing the miracles of Jesus as often as we should is due to a refusal to exercise simple childlike faith. To say it another way, we have placed limits on our faith that God never intended. Like the Galatian church, we have been bewitched into believing that we are lacking something. We have been convinced that we need more philosophy and more mechanics. Essentially, we have moved away from the simplicity of the gospel of Christ.

By works I am not referring to action, but to the works of the law described in Galatians 3. I am speaking of formulas and methodologies that we create out of a sense of pride and self-righteousness. The reason why so many people don't see miracles is because they are focusing on the wrong thing; they are focusing on themselves! It is not about your ability or your goodness; it is about His unlimited power at work in you. I should also address another issue that hinders the believer from flowing in God's miraculous power: selfish ambition. It is not about us being exalted! Take the pressure off yourself and put it where it belongs—on Him! Simply believe, and you will experience the manifestation of God's supernatural power. You already have the faith!

A TESTIMONY OF FAITH

One day we had a prayer meeting at our house. A lady came in who had suffered severe damage from a car accident several years prior. As a result of this accident, she had a series of pins and rods placed in her hip, knee, and ankle. This metal caused her to walk with a limp. The doctors told her that she would never be able to run, wear heels, or engage in any athletic activity ever again. While in worship, the Spirit of God prompted me to pray over her (I was sensitive to His voice). I declared that the fire of God touch her from the crown of her head to the soles of her feet. As I was praying for her, she felt the fire of God all over her body. As this experience took place, she began releasing her faith for a miracle. She screamed and cried out for nearly 30 minutes or more, non-stop.

After this experience, she got up from the floor and went her way. Two days later, during a book-signing event I had at a Christian bookstore, this woman came into the store with full workout gear on and a smile on her face. She explained to me that she had just finished running nine miles. Did you hear what I just said? Praise God! I was amazed. Two days earlier she could hardly walk; now she was running without any pain at all. She showed us four pages of X-rays illustrating the metal in her body. We believe that God turned the metal in her body into bone. Glory to God! I want to bring out the fact that I did not do anything except exercise faith and follow the leading of the Holy Spirit. It had nothing to do with human effort. If God will use me to turn metal into bone, I believe that He will do the same for you and greater!

The moment you became born again, you had all the faith you needed for miracles.

IT'S ALREADY IN YOU!

Years ago, I heard an African proverb which states, *"Wetin dey for Sokoto, e dey for shokoto!"* (This is pigeon English.) This old adage means, "Why are you going all the way to the city for what is already in your pants' pocket?" Simply put, you already have it in you. Many people are traveling to every conference in the world, trying to find power that they already have. Christians throughout the church are praying, "Lord increase our faith!" They believe that if they had more faith God could use them. The moment you became born again, you had all the faith you needed for miracles. We will talk more about the gift of faith in a later chapter, but you must understand what you have before you can use it.

Unfortunately, modern-day, westernized Christianity has not helped things very much. The Western church has unknowingly promoted spiritual laziness and spectatorship. We look to our church leaders to do all the work. They are the ones seen as men and women of great faith and power. Though I love to celebrate the faith and accomplishments of men and women in the body of Christ, I believe there is a healthy balance. When this admiration becomes a means of causing the body of Christ to become stagnant, we are missing the mark.

The truth is that you are already a man or woman of great faith, even though you may not realize it yet. God wants you to experience all His Kingdom has to offer, here and now! Stop waiting for more faith. Stop waiting for an impartation. Titles are great, but the power of God does not rest in titles. The power of God comes from believing the Word of God. What if I told you that the miracle you were looking for was one step of faith away? When the preacher told you that Jesus was Lord, you took a step of faith. That same step of faith is all that is required to begin walking in God's supernatural power; this includes signs, wonders, miracles, and divine provision. Everything you need and desire to experience in the Christian life is released by faith.

AN EXERCISE IN HEARING

Several years ago, I embarked on a missions trip to Haiti. This was shortly after the devastating earthquake in 2010. The nation was still ravaged and suffering from severe infrastructural damage. We were traveling to a remote village in Port-de-Paix (a small city in the Haitian mountains) to preach the Gospel and feed over 400 children.

Due to the severely damaged roads, a one way trip (up the mountain) that would normally take four hours took us over ten hours. On the way up the mountain, our SUV went completely dead. There was not one mechanic or gas station in sight for 60 miles or more. To make matters worse, the sun was setting soon, and the roads were very dangerous at night. What in heaven were we going to do?

Looking around, I realized that we had no tools to fix the vehicle and no one to help us. As time passed, many of the missionaries started panicking and complaining, "This is horrible!" "We are stuck!" they shouted. The moment I was about to join the complainers, the Holy Spirit spoke to me and told me to worship in front of the vehicle. This did not make any sense, but because we didn't have any other option, I obeyed. I and two other missionaries began to sing songs of worship and praise to the Lord, thanking Him for restoring our vehicle. We sang so long that we forgot about the mechanical problems altogether. The more we sang of God's awesome power, the more our faith rose. All of a sudden the engine returned to life. Hallelujah! We danced and shouted and thanked the Lord for His miraculous power. We did not realize that we already had the power of God in us to address the situation. That power simply needed to be released by faith.

In the same way, many people are waiting for something to happen before they will move in faith. Maybe you are waiting to finish Bible school or achieve some great level of spirituality before you will act on your faith. My friend, this is a mistake! It is time for you to take a step of faith. Do something you have never done before! Believe God for that which you have never believed before. Don't be afraid! You already have the ingredients inside you.

FAITH DECLARATION

*Father, in the **name** of **Jesus,** I thank You for who You are and all that You have done. I declare in the name of*

*Jesus Christ that I have intimacy with the Holy Spirit, and through this intimacy I walk in the miraculous. I hear the voice of the Holy Spirit on a consistent basis. I am Your sheep and I hear Your voice, Lord. I will not listen or respond to the voice of a stranger. I can discern the voice of the Lord. I hear from You clearly regarding major decisions in my life. I receive strategic direction from the Holy Spirit as it relates to my finances, relationships, choices, occupation, calling, witnessing, and every other area in my life. As a result of this **spiritual hearing,** I have **great faith** in Your Word. I love to hear the voice of the Spirit. I decree that every voice in my life that is not the voice of the Holy Spirit is silenced right now in Jesus's name!*

7

Ever-Increasing Faith

For therein is the righteousness of God revealed from faith to faith: as it is written, The just shall live by faith (Romans 1:17 KJV).

We have seen so far that the believer has already been given "the measure of faith." This faith is given to us at the moment we are saved; it is a gift of God's grace. We also discovered that this faith must be developed through meditating on (and obeying) God's Word and becoming sensitive to the Holy Spirit.

You may have been under the impression that you don't have enough faith, but this impression is not true according to the Bible. Faith is like a seed planted in the ground. Once the seed of faith is deposited in your spirit, God intends for it to grow and mature. In fact, the Bible says that the righteousness of God is revealed from faith to faith (see Romans 1:17). What does this mean? It means that the more God reveals Himself, the more your faith grows, and the more your faith grows, the more you see the righteousness of God manifested in your life. Simply put, the more you believe, the more you will see (referring to spiritual revelation), and the more you see, the more you will believe. This is the Kingdom pattern of ever-increasing faith. If you have been a believer for any length of time, your faith should not be at the same level it was when you first became a Christian. Your faith should always be increasing and maturing, daily. This is a natural process for the born-again believer.

Remember, the Christian life is not static; you are either going forward or going backward. You are either growing in faith or growing in doubt. The Bible says that the just shall live by faith. You have been justified in Christ; therefore you are to live by faith. God never intended for us to live by our five senses or by human philosophy. We live by faith! When the Bible says that the just shall "live" by faith, it uses the Greek word *zaō,* which means to have true life, worthy of its name. This is a life of power and vigor that accurately depicts God's original intent for the Christian life. The Christian life is a life of supernatural power. Faith is the means by which we release that supernatural power.

 This is why meditating on the Word is so important when it comes to developing your faith, because you cannot exercise real faith beyond your knowledge of God's will.

For instance, there are times when we have to believe God for His supernatural provision in our lives. We start out by trusting God as our provider. It may be a debt that needs cancelling or a financial obligation that needs paying. Once you exercise faith in this area and see God manifest Himself, your faith goes to another level of strength and veracity. Now you are more confident the next time you face a similar challenge. This is why meditating on the Word is so important when it comes to developing your faith, because you cannot exercise real faith beyond your knowledge of God's will. Many people find it hard to trust God, because they are ignorant of His will. How do you discover what the will of God is? Simple! The Word of God is the will of God. If you want to have confidence in His will, familiarize yourself with His Word.

FAITH FOR SUPERNATURAL PROVISION

There was a time when I lived under absolute financial bondage. I was so broke that I couldn't even pay attention (at least that is what I thought at the time). I loved the Lord, attended church regularly, and gave tithes from time to time. "Lord, why am I suffering?" I exclaimed. The truth was, I was completely ignorant concerning God's will for my finances. Early in my walk with Christ, I was told that prosperity preachers were bad and that their message should be shunned. I allowed a few bad apples to spoil my bunch (so to speak). An amazing thing happened one day. As I was reading the Word of God, I came across a verse in 2 Corinthians:

> *And God is able to make all grace abound toward you, that you, **always having all sufficiency in all things**, may have an abundance for every good work* (2 Corinthians 9:8).

I could not get the phrase "always having all sufficiency in all things" out of my mind. What did this phrase mean? When I looked it up in my Bible concordance, I found out that this phrase literally means that God wants us in a perfect state of life, where we are in need of *no aid or support*. Simply put, He doesn't want us begging for resources, trapped in debt, or dependent on government assistance. Essentially, it was outside of the will of God for me to live in constant financial struggle.

In my search for greater truth, I read hundreds of scriptures in the Bible on finances and they all said the same thing—God wanted me blessed! At this point, I changed my attitude. Instead of settling for lack and insufficiency, I began to declare that I was blessed. My prayer life changed. No longer would I allow the enemy to rob me of the promises of God in my life. I started to give to the Lord the way His Word says I should.

I prayed the prayer of faith: "God, I thank You for your supernatural provision at work in my life. I declare that I have no need of aid or support, but I have all sufficiency in all things." A miraculous thing took place in that very moment. My faith rose up inside of me, and I began to believe God in the area of finances. Soon after, resources began to flow from every direction. A revelation of the will of God, coupled with appropriate corresponding action, resulted in financial breakthrough. Today I consistently live in the blessings of God.

Why do I share this story? Until I had a revelation of the will of God for my life, I could not believe God for more. Your faith will never go beyond your revelation of His will. It all started with me taking a step of faith based on the Word of God. You may be struggling today. You may be saying to yourself, "Things will never get better!" My friend, you are one step of faith away from your breakthrough. Don't give in to your feelings; release your faith and you will see the manifestation of God in your life.

THERE IS MORE!

Years ago, a pastor I know personally was holding a meeting in Nigeria. This was a small crusade. People from the surrounding villages came to hear the Gospel of Jesus Christ. The goal was to evangelize the area. There were several pastors involved in this crusade, and many of them had an opportunity to teach and preach. As they proclaimed the resurrected Christ, people came to the altar in the hundreds to give their lives to Jesus.

After the crusade was over, the pastors gathered in their quarters. As they were praying, a woman came to them with a dead baby in her arms. This was her youngest child. The little boy had been dead for hours. She said to the pastors, "You say that Jesus is real, so I brought my baby to you so that you could ask Jesus to raise him from the dead." The pastors were perplexed. None of them had any experience raising the dead. What were they going to do? They began to pray. As they prayed, absolutely nothing happened. The more they prayed, the more discouraged they became. The child remained in the same cold, lifeless state.

While everyone was looking around, one of the pastors had a word of wisdom—worship. The Lord told them to simply worship Him. So they placed the baby in the middle of the floor, made a circle around him, and began to worship. This worship went on for six hours straight. All of a sudden they heard what sounded like a cough. As they looked down on the floor, the baby began to make sounds and wiggle. Eventually, the baby came to life and began crying. Glory to God! These weren't some huge mega church pastors with mega faith. They were average men who dared to believe God. They knew in their hearts that there was more.

I am here to tell you that there is more! How desperate are you to see the Kingdom of God manifested on earth as it is in heaven? The same God who saves your soul and heals your body is the same God who raises the dead. Those pastors simply listened to the Spirit of God. You may think that miracles only happen to certain people in certain places. That is a myth! Miracles happen to anyone who will believe God.

A TESTIMONY OF FAITH

A woman contacted us with a prayer request for cancer. The doctor found cancerous cells in her bloodstream. They immediately gave her a negative diagnosis. She cried to God in desperation and reached out to our ministry for prayer and encouragement. God led us to curse the cancer in her body and to command it to cease and desist. Upon returning to the physician, the X-rays indicated that there was not a single trace of cancer in her blood. Thank You, Jesus!

The Word of God says in Exodus 23:25, "So you shall serve the Lord your God, and He will bless your bread and your water. And I will take sickness away from the midst of you." This tells us that the will of God was not for that woman to have cancer, but for her to be well; therefore, we cursed the cancer by the roots. It was a simple act of faith, which yielded an exponential return. The woman was completely healed! The truth is that you no longer have to settle for less than what God has made available to you! Once you know what the Word of God says, you can point your faith in that direction. The more you hear about and experience these kinds of miracles, the more your faith will grow.

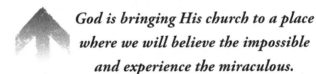

God is bringing His church to a place where we will believe the impossible and experience the miraculous.

Remember, God doesn't want you to remain stagnant. He wants your faith to transcend limitations. He wants you to believe Him at the level He reveals Himself. Have you ever wondered why He allowed the disciples to witness His resurrection? God knew that if they were going to spread the Gospel and expand the church, they needed to know without equivocation that He could do anything. The same stands true of you and me today. God is bringing His church to a place where we will believe the impossible and experience the miraculous.

FAITH IS AN ACTION WORD

*But do you want to know, O foolish man, that faith
without works is dead?* (James 2:20)

The Bible tells us that without faith it is impossible to please God.
I want to reiterate the fact that everything in the Christian life hinges
upon faith. With that being said, it is important to know that faith is
an action word. Faith always motivates action! In the book of James,
chapter 2, Apostle James tells us "faith without works is dead." What
does this expression mean? Earlier I mentioned that walking in the
supernatural was not a matter of performing religious works. This
statement is true, but this is not the "works" that James is referring to.
In this passage, the Bible is referring to corresponding action. In other
words, faith without corresponding action is rendered powerless.

We know that faith requires confessing the Word of God, but we
must also do that which we are confessing. I can't tell you how many
people I have ministered to and prayed for who have neglected this
simple truth. They are waiting for God to do something, when in
reality God is waiting for them to act. By this I am not referring to
the old adage, "God helps those who help themselves." I am referring
to you moving in the direction of your faith. Simply put, you must
act on what you believe. For example, if you believe God to heal your
body, the first step is to believe that God is the Healer. The next step
is to confess His healing promises over your life, and the third step is
to start acting like one who is already healed (along with your regular
visits to the physician). Without that third step, you will be confessing forever and a day without any results. To illustrate this truth, I
want to share a scripture with you:

*Now Peter and John went up together to the temple at the
hour of prayer, the ninth hour. And a certain man lame*

from his mother's womb was carried, whom they laid daily at the gate of the temple which is called Beautiful, to ask alms from those who entered the temple; who, seeing Peter and John about to go into the temple, asked for alms. And fixing his eyes on him, with John, Peter said, "Look at us." So he gave them his attention, expecting to receive something from them. Then Peter said, "Silver and gold I do not have, but what I do have I give you: In the name of Jesus Christ of Nazareth, rise up and walk." And he took him by the right hand and lifted him up, and immediately his feet and ankle bones received strength. So he, leaping up, stood and walked and entered the temple with them—walking, leaping, and praising God (Acts 3:1-8).

Here we see that Peter gave the word to "rise up and walk." This was a word of faith. As the lame man laid hold of this word, the Bible says that Peter grabbed him by the hand, and immediately his anklebones received strength (notice that Peter took action). The most critical component is highlighted in verse 8: "So he, leaping up, stood and walked and entered the temple with them—walking, leaping, and praising God." What happened to this lame man? He clearly received a miracle; however, this miracle was not without his participation. In order to receive this miracle, he had to *act* on his faith. How did he act on his faith? By walking! You must step out on your faith if you want to see manifestation.

I love the word *walk* in this passage; it comes from the Greek word *peripateō*, and it means to make due use of an opportunity. The lame man didn't care about how long he had been incapacitated; he saw an opportunity and he took advantage of it. He took the initiative and acted on what he believed. We see the same kind of faith in the case of Abraham and his son Isaac. God told Abraham to sacrifice his only son, and because he trusted God he obeyed, knowing that God would raise him from the dead if necessary to fulfill His promise (see Hebrews 11:19). That is what I call *faith in action*. Ultimately, God sent a ram in Isaac's place.

The point is that you and I have to act on our faith. The more you act on your faith, the more your faith will grow and the stronger it will become. The more your faith grows, the more it will facilitate the miraculous demonstration of the Spirit of God. Faith is the revelation of God's Word in action, therefore we must be doers of the Word and not hearers only! (See James 1:22.) Faith must have a corresponding action (we mentioned earlier that the first corresponding action of faith is confessing the Word). By acting on the Word of God, we are becoming more and more conscious of His power and ability. We are removing the limits and the excuses.

If you want to see a miracle, start looking for a miracle and acting on the Word every opportunity you get. It is just that simple. We must refuse to have a passive attitude toward the things of God. This begins with our decision to step out of ourselves and rest in His power. Oftentimes we hear great sermons on Sunday morning and never put them into practice. Do something! Say something! Move out of your comfort zone. If you will do this consistently, I guarantee you will begin to walk in the realm of the miraculous.

FAITH DECLARATION

*Father, in the **name** of Jesus, I thank You for who You are and all that You have done in my life. I declare that my faith is increasing daily. Today I declare and confess in the name of Jesus Christ that I have great faith. I declare that mountains of fear, doubt, and worry are removed from me and cast into the sea because I believe Your Word. I walk in the power of the Holy Spirit on a consistent basis. I am not moved by circumstances in my life, but I have decided* *to believe. Faith is the revelation of Your Word in action; therefore I am a doer of your Word and not a hearer only. As You direct me, I will demonstrate Your Kingdom and power every opportunity I get. In the name of Jesus! Amen!*

8

DEMAND AND SUPPLY

"Bring all the tithes into the storehouse, that there may be food in My house, and try Me now in this," says the Lord of hosts, "If I will not open for you the windows of heaven and pour out for you such blessing that there will not be room enough to receive it" (MALACHI 3:10).

GROWING UP IN THE SOUTH, I CAN REMEMBER MY GRANDMOTHER'S house. In the back yard there was an old hand well. Before the times of faucet water in America, people would pump water from the well. This was often a very difficult task. It required great upper body strength and patience. This system functioned based on a concept called demand and supply. These pumps were usually made from cast iron and involved drawing water from a well underground through a spout on the surface. The more you pumped, the more water would flow. Even if it didn't look like anything was coming out, you had to keep pumping; it would eventually come to the surface. In many ways, the life of faith is very similar to pumping a hand well. You must place a demand on the Word of God by faith. The more you demand, the more miraculous power will be supplied.

In my studies of the first and second Great Awakening in American history, I discovered that individuals who had enough audacity to place a demand on the Word of God sparked these revivals. We stated before that the Word of God contains the latent power of God. Like a sponge soaked with water, the moment you squeeze the sponge water will gush out. The world needs to see a demonstration of the Spirit of God like never before. The darker the days become, the more desperate we must become for the Kingdom of God to be revealed in great power and manifestation. We must make the demand in order for heaven to supply.

I am no longer content with relishing the past; there must be a new and fresh move of the Spirit of God in this generation. I believe that we are on the edge of one of the greatest revivals we have ever seen in human history. The cosmos is groaning in anticipation for the manifestation of the sons of God. All of this begins with you and me placing an effectual demand on heaven. Many people think that placing a demand on God's Word is a negative thing. This is not true at all. In fact, the Lord tells us to prove Him (see Malachi 3:10). The book of Matthew further illustrates this truth:

> *And when the men of that place recognized Him, they sent out into all that surrounding region, brought to Him all who were sick, and begged Him that they might only touch the hem of His garment. And as many as touched it were made perfectly well* (Matthew 14:35-36).

This is a perfect illustration of what happens when you place a demand on the Word of God. The Bible says that when the men of the city heard that Jesus had come, they sent out into all the country and gathered the sick. They knew that if they could simply touch the hem of His garment, they would be made whole. This is exactly what took place! What is the spiritual significance of this scripture? The word *hem* is actually the Greek word *kraspedon* and it literally means tassel or tuft. This tassel was a common appendage to the tallit (a Jewish prayer shawl, very prominent during the time of Christ). The tassel on the edge of the tallit represented the Torah. Most Jewish people during the time of Christ were familiar with this concept. Essentially, the people were not just grabbing hold of the extension of Jesus's garment, but they were literally placing a demand on the promises of God's Word for healing and wholeness symbolically represented in the prayer shawl of the Messiah. I believe that as they touched Jesus in faith, the healing power of God was released. The Bible says that "as many" as touched Him were made whole. The more they demanded, the more they received a supply.

THE SPIRITUAL LAW OF DEMAND

When we talk about demand, we are not simply talking about some spiritual ritual, but we are talking about a spiritual law that has very powerful implications. The more you learn to place a fervent demand on the Word, the more you will see miracles. This is powerfully expressed in Luke's Gospel: "So I say to you, ask, and it will be given to you; seek, and you will find; knock, and it will be opened to you" (Luke 11:9). This spiritual principle is displayed all throughout the Bible. If you want something you have to ask.

The more you learn to place a fervent demand on the Word, the more you will see miracles.

Imagine you were related to the wealthiest businessman in the world and you needed financial capital to start your business. Would you keep quiet? If you never make the need known, you will never

THE POWER OF UNLIMITED FAITH

receive the resources that you require. The same is true in the spiritual realm. If you don't place a faith demand on the promises of God's Word, you will never see those promises come to fruition in your life or the lives of your loved ones.

We place a demand on the promises of God through the prayer of faith (we will speak further on this later). We must ask God in faith in order to receive the promises of God. Let us consider some of these promises. John 14:12 says, "Most assuredly, I say to you, he who believes in Me, the works that I do he will do also; and greater *works* than these he will do, because I go to My Father." This passage is a conservative theologian's nightmare. Why? Jesus said that the person who believes in Him would do the same things that He did and greater. You can't explain this passage away! This would have to include healing the sick, raising the dead, casting out devils, and manifesting the miraculous.

FAITH RELEASES THE GREATER WORKS

Remember, you cannot exercise faith beyond your knowledge of the will of God. Jesus said that it is the will of God for us to do the same things He did and *greater*. Now that you know that this is the will of God, it is time for you to place a demand on it by faith. The question is not, "What would Jesus do?" The question is, "What *did* Jesus do?" When you leave the house, ask yourself, "What miracle is God going to do through me today?" This is what faith is all about: simply placing a demand on the Word of God.

Some would say, "Well, Jesus didn't really mean that!" What did He mean then? Statements like that are meant to neutralize your faith and confine you to the natural realm. Instead of making excuses, start placing a demand. Give God a try! He longs to show you how real He is. Besides the promise of doing what Jesus did, we are told that if we "ask" we shall receive. What do you desire from the Lord today?

Have you asked Him yet? What are you waiting for? The Bible says that anything that we ask "in His name" (in His authority, character, and power) will be done for us. The writer of this text uses the Greek pronoun *hostis,* which means whatever or whoever. The last time I checked, whoever or whatever included you and me. Whatever you are willing to ask for in faith, God is willing to give. If that doesn't make you excited, you may need to check your pulse! The time is now to start believing God for the impossible.

THE SPIRITUAL LAW OF SUPPLY

It is very important to understand that we are, first and foremost, spiritual beings, and as such we are supplied with supernatural resources from the realm of the Spirit. The Bible tells us that God is the Father of spirits (see Hebrews 12:9). Jesus Himself stated that we are sustained by the Word of God and not just physical bread (see Luke 4:4). If you are going to receive a supply, you need to know where to place the demand. Just as the hand well that I spoke of earlier, you have to learn to focus your time and energy in the right place if you are going to get the supply that you need. When pumping a hand well, you have to put all your energy on the lever and not the spout. What do I mean by this? The lever represents the spiritual realm and the spout represents the natural realm. Every time you pull the lever, you are creating motion underneath the surface that will ultimately cause something to pour out of the spout, even when you can't see activity above the surface. Keep pumping!

In the same manner, it may not seem like anything is taking place in the natural, but keep confessing your faith and obeying the Word. Eventually, it will bring the manifestation that you are looking for. In the Kingdom of God, things take place in the unseen realm before they are manifested in the natural. The Holy Spirit is responsible for bringing manifestation. One day as I was praying, I heard the

Spirit of God say to me, "Kynan, the reason why you are frustrated is because you are trying to do My job. Your job is to do the believing, and My job is to do the manifesting." Wow! Prior to that time, I never considered this truth. I didn't realize that by trying to do the manifesting (through my own human effort) I was no longer walking by faith.

Once you engage God based on His Word, He is obligated to move mightily on your behalf.

So many people are struggling and toiling when the reality is that God doesn't need our help; He simply wants us to believe Him so that He can manifest Himself in every circumstance of our lives. He is the supplier, and the more you and I acknowledge Him for who He is, the more we will be able to experience the blessing, breakthrough, and supernatural provision He has ordained. Once you engage God based on His Word, He is obligated to move mightily on your behalf. That is right! I said that God is obligated according to Psalm 138:2, "For You have magnified Your word above all Your name." God has committed Himself to His Word in a way that you and I would find difficult to comprehend with the natural mind. Remember, God and His Word are one (see John 1:1-3). Therefore, He must perform what His Word declares. We have to make up in our mind that His Word is the final authority in our lives, and once we do we can speak it forth with power and authority.

RIVERS OF SUPERNATURAL POWER

He who believes in Me, as the Scripture has said, out of his heart will flow rivers of living water (John 7:38).

I believe the analogy of the well is fitting, because it is the perfect picture of how you and I are to walk in the power of God, and see the Kingdom manifested on earth as it is in heaven. It does not matter whether it is healing, deliverance, financial provision, or some other miracle, God wants us to experience His power and know that He is real. The Bible says, "He who believes in Me, as the Scripture has said, out of his heart will flow rivers of living water." What does this really mean?

First, let us define the word *heart* (more accurately translated *belly*). This is the Greek word *koilia* and it means innermost being. This is the deep recesses of our inner man. Simply put, this is your spirit man. We found out earlier that the power of God is already resident within us. The Bible goes further to say that from our innermost being will flow "rivers" of living water. This river is not some small little stream; the Bible uses the Greek word *potamos,* which literally means torrent. A torrent is defined as a strong and fast-moving stream, a deluge or overflow. Amazing! Did you know that there was a supernatural torrent stirring in your inward man? God has deposited so much power in you that you are literally bursting at the seams. Therefore, if you are looking for supernatural power, you need only look within because the Holy Spirit lives inside you.

There is a well inside you that is ready to be released; you simply need to draw from it by faith. It is almost offensive to think that all we have to do is place a demand on God by faith, but that is exactly what we must do. You may say, "But I prayed and nothing happened!" Is that a reason to quit? Keep placing a demand and you will find yourself overtaken by a deluge of the miraculous. You have to want more to get more! How desperate are you?

FAITH DECLARATION

Father, in the precious name of Your Son Jesus, I now declare that Your miracle working power operates freely in every area of my life. According to the spiritual law of demand, I now place a demand on the promises of Your Word. I declare that my "well" is full and overflowing with Your miraculous power. I thank You, Father, that Your rivers of supernatural power flow in and through me. According to John 14:12, I am empowered to do the same works as Jesus and greater. Thank You, Holy Spirit, for opening my mind and spirit to the deeper realms of the supernatural; in the name of Jesus. Amen!

9

KINGDOM CURRENCY

*Ho! Everyone who thirsts, Come to the waters;
and you who have no money, Come, buy and
eat. Yes, come, buy wine and milk without
money and without price* (ISAIAH 55:1).

ON MY FIRST TRIP TO AFRICA, I CAN REMEMBER OUR GUIDE TAKING us to a very busy marketplace. Here we were told that we could exchange our U.S. dollars for foreign currency. This would enable us to transact while we were in Africa. There was a significant difference in value between the currency that I held (dollars) and the local currency. Currency is very important to any economy. Without it, you cannot transact business. Faith is the currency of the Kingdom of God, and without it we cannot transact in the spiritual realm. By currency, I am referring to a system of money or legal tender used in a particular country. If you travel to Nigeria (for example) and visit the local market there, the vendor will quote prices in naira and not dollars (with some exceptions).

If you travel to the United Kingdom you will have to convert to pounds or euros.

The point is that every country has a currency. Faith is the spiritual currency or medium of exchange by which we obtain what we need from the heavenly realm. This is why the Bible says in Hebrews 11, "But without faith, it is impossible to please God." It doesn't matter how much people murmur or complain, without approaching God with faith (the currency He accepts) they will not be able to receive from Him. Have you ever been to a market or grocery store? What takes place in that environment? You pick the things that you need or want, and you bring them to the clerk. Once the clerk has calculated the total cost of your items, you exchange some medium with the clerk in order to satisfy the cost of your goods. If a person would attempt to buy something from the market without money, the person would be considered a thief.

However, the Bible says in Isaiah 55:1 (KJV), "Ho, everyone that thirsteth, come ye to the waters, and he that hath no money; come ye, buy, and eat; yea, come, buy wine and milk without money and without price." What is God saying in this passage? How do you buy something without money and without price? Essentially, God is not looking for our physical money and what He has to offer is priceless, but He wants us to approach Him with faith and confidence; and by doing so, we will release that which He has made available to us. This is a spiritual transaction. Physical things cannot buy spiritual things. You can't buy His blessings, but you can receive them by faith. We will talk a little later about how this transaction takes place, but for now I want to go a little deeper into the economy of God.

THE ECONOMY OF GOD

In college, I took a course in macroeconomics. There I learned of the concept of an economy. An economy is the wealth and resources of a nation and the system by which that wealth is managed, with the idea that resources are limited or scarce. There are three components to almost every market economy; these are called factors of production, which consist of land, labor, and capital. Land is defined as the raw materials and natural resources that are present in an economic system (gold, oil, trees, et cetera). Labor is defined as the human resources in an economy (workers involved in converting resources into goods and services). Capital is defined as the machinery, factories, and equipment used in producing goods and services. These goods and services are then bought and sold on an open market, thus meeting the needs and wants of those within that market. All of these factors work together to facilitate an efficient and healthy economy.

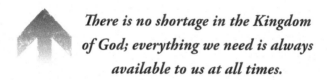

There is no shortage in the Kingdom of God; everything we need is always available to us at all times.

We are citizens of the Kingdom of God. The Kingdom of God is the most efficient economic system in the universe. Why? Because God is the ultimate Economist and His economy is filled with unlimited resources. There is no shortage in the Kingdom of God; everything we need is always available to us at all times. In any economic system, you must place a demand on the resources available in order to benefit from them. The economy of God is no different. The problem is that most people are ignorant of God's economy (the system that governs God's unlimited resources in heaven and earth).

What does any of this have to do with faith? We said earlier that faith was the currency of God's Kingdom. In other words, you and I must pull from the unlimited resources of heaven by faith. By resources, I am not simply referring to money—I am talking about whatever we need in any given situation. For example, someone may need a kidney transplant or a heart transplant. Did you know that

God is the Supreme Manufacturer and Supplier of body parts? Every supplier has an inventory of excess parts and supplies. What makes you think that heaven doesn't have an inventory of hearts, legs, eyes, and kidneys that are ready to be distributed to the body of Christ?

Remember, heaven has no shortage! There are people in the body of Christ suffering because they won't place a demand on heaven's supply. The Bible says that the very hairs on our head are numbered; that means that God keeps inventory of every aspect of His creation. He is the Greatest Entrepreneur in the world. You may not have looked at things from this vantage point, but it is absolutely true. How do we access heaven's inventory? The same way you access any inventory; you have to place an order (or make a demand). This is done through the prayer of faith.

THE FERVENT PRAYER OF FAITH

Confess your trespasses to one another, and pray for one another, that you may be healed. The effective, fervent prayer of a righteous man avails much (James 5:16).

Now that we know that God has a Kingdom economy, and faith is the currency of this Kingdom, we can begin placing a demand on the power of God through faith. More specifically, you and I have to learn to pray the prayer of faith. The Bible says in James chapter 5 that the prayer of faith will save the sick (see James 5:15). This is powerful! You may think that prayer is not that important, but you would be mistaken. Prayer is powerful. In fact, prayer is so powerful that it can raise a sick person from a bed of affliction, open blinded eyes, and bring deliverance.

The key to seeing results from our prayers is to pray in faith. The Bible calls this the "effectual fervent prayer." What does this term mean? The word *effectual* is the Greek word *energeo*, which means to be operative or to "put forth power." In other words, there must be Kingdom currency behind our prayers. This faith currency is what gives power and energy to our prayer life. If someone wants to make a transaction in the natural realm, there must be enough currency to support that transaction. In the same manner, when you and I want to experience the supernatural our lives, we must have the appropriate currency to make the transaction. You can't use jellybeans to purchase a car. Why? It is not the appropriate medium of exchange. We must approach God the right way if we want to get results, and the right way is to approach Him in faith. When we learn to pray in faith, it will "avail much" (bring manifestation). The Bible says in James 5:17-18 (KJV):

> *Elias was a man subject to like passions as we are, and he prayed earnestly that it might not rain: and it rained not on the earth by the space of three years and six months. And he prayed again, and the heaven gave rain, and the earth brought forth her fruit.*

Here we see that Elisha prayed "earnestly" that it would not rain on the earth, and for three years and six months there was not a single drop of rain. How could this be? Elisha didn't come up with theological barriers to his prayer request. He didn't make excuses. Contrariwise, the prophet chose to believe that God could do anything. As a result of this fervent prayer of faith, heaven responded.

The beauty of this passage is that God is no respecter of persons. The Bible highlights that he was a man of "like passions" or weaknesses. What He did for Elisha, He will do for us. What is the key? The key is praying fervently. Another way to express this truth is, you must pray with *all* your heart. You must believe that there are no other alternatives. There is no contingency plan! The problem in our modern culture is that we have too many alternatives. If we feel sick we can take pills or go to the doctor. If we run out of money we can get loans from the bank or a family member, and if our children are unruly we can take them to a counselor. We have been taught (especially in Western culture) to depend on everything else but God.

What would happen if one day all of our support systems were removed? Would you still be able to trust God? Beloved, the time is coming when the systems of this world will be shaken. In that day we will have no other choice but to trust God. Don't wait until that time comes; trust God *today!* Take the limits off of your faith by taking the limits off of God. He can do anything! Every miracle and supernatural manifestation recorded in the Bible is yours for the taking. It is time out for passivity and fear. Be bold! Dare to believe God without reservation. Heaven is ready to supply whatever your faith is willing to demand. Faith is the currency that you need to make this spiritual transaction.

OUR HEAVENLY ACCOUNT

Not that I seek the gift, but I seek the fruit that abounds to your account. And my God shall supply all your need according to His riches in glory by Christ Jesus (Philippians 4:17,19).

One of my favorite books of the Bible is the book of Philippians. Paul actually wrote this epistle from house arrest (according to most scholars). In this epistle, Apostle Paul encourages the Philippian church to put their faith in God, and he lauds them for supporting him financially.

In the fourth chapter of Philippians, Paul makes a very interesting statement. He thanks the church for helping him in his financial need and tells them that he doesn't desire their financial gift, but "fruit that may abound to their account." What does he mean by this statement? By investing in Paul's ministry they were actually receiving credit to their "heavenly account." This is a profound truth! We actually have an account in heaven. I believe that the Philippians were receiving credit to their account, not simply due to the amount of their giving, but due to their faith.

Every act of faith and obedience to God causes a harvest of blessing to accumulate in our spiritual account.

Did you know that every believer has a heavenly account? Well, we do! In fact, Jesus put it this way: "Take heed that ye do not your alms before men, to be seen of them: otherwise ye have no reward of your Father, which is in heaven" (Matthew 6:1 KJV). The word *reward* in this passage is the Greek word *misthos,* which literally means "dues paid." Every act of faith and obedience to God causes a harvest of blessing to accumulate in our spiritual account. Remember, the realm of the spirit is of a deeper and truer reality than the realm of the natural. In other words, your heavenly account is more significant than your physical account.

Is your account full or empty? So many people invest all their energy in filling their physical bank accounts while their heavenly account has "insufficient funds." Like all accounts, you must make withdrawals if you want to access the resources contained therein. Faith is the means by which we make withdrawals from our heavenly account. Unlike natural accounts, we do not fill our heavenly account with money; we fill our account with Kingdom currency. In other words, we fill our heavenly account by faith. By faith, we make deposits in and place a demand upon our heavenly account. This is why Paul says, "My God shall supply all your need according to His riches in glory" (Philippians 4:19). God has an unlimited supply in the realm of Glory. There is no lack or shortage.

The question remains, do you have sufficient faith in your account to make the appropriate demand on heaven? *Every time you pray the prayer of faith you are making a supernatural withdrawal.* It doesn't matter how things seem in the natural. Place your faith and trust in God, no matter what! Don't look at what you see in the natural. Make a demand on heaven's resources. By doing so, you are releasing the unlimited power and miraculous provision of God in your life.

A TESTIMONY OF FAITH

One year my wife and I were expecting a newborn baby, and the vehicle we had was not big enough to accommodate our growing family. By this time we already vowed to the Lord that we would never finance another personal vehicle. Besides this, we did not have the funds (in the natural) to afford a new car. While praying one day, the Lord impressed upon my heart to ask Him for the vehicle we needed. As a result of this unction within, I decided to discuss the details of our next vehicle purchase with my wife. After several days, we agreed upon a make and model of the car (you have to be specific when asking for something). We prayed the prayer of faith, thanking God for our vehicle.

Some may think this was a silly exercise—speak for yourself! When you have a legitimate need, you must learn to approach God in faith as your loving Provider. This is exactly what we did. Week after week went by with no vehicle and our baby was due very soon. All of a sudden, one day we received the exact amount of funds we needed to pay for the vehicle *in full*. Hallelujah! We decided to put our trust in God and not look at our physical circumstances. Our heavenly account was full! We simply made a withdrawal.

FAITH DECLARATION

I declare, in Jesus's name, that I have a greater understanding and awareness of Kingdom currency. Faith is the means by which we receive the promises of Your Word; therefore I declare that I possess supernatural faith. My "heavenly account" is full because I believe and trust in Your Word above anything else. Thank You for supplying all of my needs (spirit, soul, and body) according to Your riches in glory through Christ. I am the head and not the tail. I am above only and not beneath. I position myself to experience and walk in Your miracle working power in every area of my life. Nothing shall be impossible to me from this day forward. In the name of Jesus, I declare; amen!

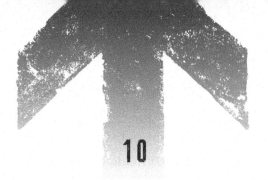

10

FAITH AND LOVE

For in Christ Jesus neither circumcision nor
uncircumcision avails anything, but faith
working through love (GALATIANS 5:6).

WE HAVE DISCOVERED MANY THINGS ABOUT FAITH, SUCH AS THE Law of Confession, the difference between faith and works, Kingdom currency, and the like. Hopefully, you have a deeper understanding at this point of what it takes to experience God's miraculous power in your life—namely unlimited faith in the Word of God. We mentioned before that faith is the key that releases the latent power of God's Word. This means that faith is one of the most important aspects of victorious Christian living. With that being stated, we must understand how faith works. The Bible tells us that faith works through love (see Galatians 5:6). What do we mean when we say that faith works through love? In the original Greek expression, faith is operated and empowered by love (Strong's G1754). The word used to describe this is *energeo,* which refers to power or "energy."

First of all, we need to understand that faith is not a dogmatic principle or some lifeless theological concept. Neither is faith a mystical philosophy. Faith is a right response to a supernatural God. Jesus is not an ancient and distant relic; He is the living and breathing King of kings and Lord of lords. He is a living person, and genuine faith is the living expression of our trust and confidence in the resurrected Christ. We trust Him as a result of our love for Him. This deep conviction is energized by the agape love of God. The more we love Him, the more we will trust Him, and the more we trust Him, the more we will experience His eternal power. This is a beautiful reality.

This is really the starting place for learning to operate in unlimited faith. The more God reveals Himself to us, the more our faith will grow and flourish. The important thing to understand is the inseparable relationship between faith and love. I believe that many people are falling short in their faith walk because they are unaware of this divine connection. God is love! This is His very nature. Everything that we receive from Him is an expression of that love. We seek Him because we love Him. This love is not just expressed vertically (between God and man), but it is most importantly expressed horizontally (man to man). If you want your faith to work the way it should, you must learn to continually walk in love.

Too many people are harboring offense, resentment, and bitterness in the body of Christ. As a result, they are unable to confidently appropriate the promises of God for their lives. You may think that you can hold hatred in your heart and still walk in the miraculous, but nothing could be further from the truth. Did you know that every promise in the Word of God is motivated by love? Ultimately, God sent His only begotten Son because of His love for this world. Miracles, signs, and wonders are no different; they are all motivated by the great love of the Father. This is why it behooves us to walk in love on a daily basis. If you really want to walk in the power of God, let this revelation sink down deep within your inner man. Love is the key!

LOVE EMPOWERS FAITH

Years ago, while driving from Ft. Lauderdale to Tampa, Florida (approximately a three-hour drive), I noticed that my car began to lose speed and power. This transpired on a very busy highway. I looked at the gauge, and it seemed as if nothing was wrong. All of a sudden, my car came to a complete halt. In my mind I wondered what the problem could be. Thankfully, my cell phone was functioning properly so I made a call to the emergency response dispatcher. The emergency vehicle arrived an hour later. Once the technician checked the vehicle, he explained to me that my car had run out of gas. I did not realize at the time, but my fuel gauge was malfunctioning. There was no way for me to know how much fuel was in the gas tank. This was such an embarrassing situation. Thank God I was able to get enough fuel from the emergency vehicle to make it to the nearest station and fill my tank.

Faith is the engine of the Christian life; through it we are able to receive everything that heaven has to offer, specifically the supernatural power of God.

What is the moral of this story? Faith is the engine of the Christian life; through it we are able to receive everything that heaven has to offer, specifically the supernatural power of God. If faith is the engine of the spiritual life, then love is the fuel. Like all engines, it doesn't matter how powerful they seem to be—without fuel, they are unable to function. In the same manner, without walking in love, our faith will never be able to function the way it should. Love is the driving force behind faith. When a person is walking in love, the person's ability to confidently stand on the Word of God is empowered. To further illustrate this point, let us consider Mark 11:23-26:

> *For assuredly, I say to you, whoever says to this mountain, "Be removed and be cast into the sea," and does not doubt in his heart, but believes that those things he says will be done, he will have whatever he says. Therefore I say to you, whatever things you ask when you pray, believe that you receive them, and you will have them. And whenever you stand praying, if you have anything against anyone, forgive him, that your Father in heaven may also forgive you your trespasses. But if you do not forgive, neither will your Father in heaven forgive your trespasses.*

Notice that Jesus tells His disciples that whatever they ask for in prayer, believing, they will receive. This is the ethos of faith—our ability to believe and trust God to manifest the impossible in our lives.

Immediately after this statement, Jesus deals with His disciples concerning the issue of forgiveness. Let us define forgiveness. Forgiveness is essentially the act of releasing and letting go. It comes from the Greek word *aphiēmi* and it means "to send away." To forgive is to release someone from their offense or trespass. This is what God did for us; He forgave us of all trespasses. What does this have to do with faith? Everything! Our ability to forgive people when they hurt or wound us is an expression of our love walk. In fact, forgiveness is the corresponding action of love in the same way confession is the corresponding action of faith. If you love someone, you can forgive them when they hurt you. This aspect of faith is critical in seeing the miraculous manifested in your life. If you can't forgive, then you are not walking in love and ultimately your "faith engine" can't function.

Unfortunately, I have encountered too many Christians who are bound by hurt, depression, and even sickness because they refuse to release their offender. Why? The faith that they need to exercise in order to receive breakthrough has been rendered inoperative. Like a car engine without fuel, they have come to a devastating halt in their spiritual lives. Remember, belief occurs in the heart (the repository of thoughts, desires, and decisions), and if the heart is imprisoned to resentment, bitterness, or even hatred, our ability to exercise unlimited faith can be "limited."

You may be saying to yourself, "I didn't know that this was about forgiving people!" Well now you know! If you are serious about walking in the power of God, you must make a decision to walk in love. Don't sacrifice your spiritual power for offense. The love of God is already inside you. The Holy Spirit has already shed that love abroad in your heart. Now it is time to release and let go. The more you do this, the more you will be empowered to walk in the miraculous dimension of the Christian life.

WALKING IN LOVE AND COMPASSION

Therefore be imitators of God as dear children. And walk in love, as Christ also has loved us and given Himself for us, an offering and a sacrifice to God for a sweet-smelling aroma (Ephesians 5:1-2).

We must realize that love is not an option for a believer. It is our spiritual DNA, inextricably woven within the fabric of the born-again life. A Christian who doesn't walk in love is like wind without air. Even though walking in the love of God is our spiritual nature, we must make a conscious decision to do so. The average church-goer underestimates the supernatural power of love, especially when it comes to walking in faith. Paul says in 1 Corinthians 13 that without love we are nothing. He goes further to say that love will never fail. If you and I realized the profound power of love, we would make sure that we are walking in love at all times.

I don't know about you, but I am absolutely determined to experience heaven on earth, and the only way to do that is to be an imitator of God. Jesus modeled this reality during His earthly ministry. The Bible says, *"And when Jesus went out He saw a great multitude; and He was moved with compassion for them, and healed their sick"* (Matthew 14:14). Notice that the miracle of healing was a by-product of compassion. This is the Greek word *splagchnizomai,* which means to be "moved in one's bowels" or "seat of love." Compassion is the divine ability to empathize with the pain and suffering of others. Jesus always walked in compassion. This is why He could consistently see miracles, because He was deeply concerned with releasing the people of God from demonic bondage through the power of the Spirit. Compassion is one of the key ingredients to walking in the faith for miracles, signs, and wonders. If that is not enough incentive, I should remind you that we are commanded by God Himself to love one another.

Compassion is one of the key ingredients to walking in the faith for miracles, signs, and wonders.

What do I mean when I say love? Unfortunately, we have been tremendously affected by worldly philosophies when it comes to our understanding of love. The word for "love" found in Ephesians 5 is the Greek word *agape.* This is most accurately defined as affection, goodwill, and benevolence. This means that we are walking in benevolence toward God and our fellow man and woman.

LOVE: THE POWER SOURCE

Love does not mean that we always agree, but it does mean that we are reflecting the nature of Christ in our thoughts, speech, and actions toward one another. We are called by God to live on a higher plane of reality. The more we learn to live this way, the more we will be able to believe God for the impossible. There is a cyclical relationship between faith and love; when we are walking in love, we are able to believe and trust God, and when we believe and trust God, we are able to love. The Church has preoccupied herself with slander, judgmentalism, and gossip. Many Christian news outlets have become nothing more than spiritual tabloids. We expend a tremendous amount of energy on finding the latest scandal in the Christian community and broadcasting it to the world, rather than restoring our fallen brothers and sisters in the faith. This is not the love of God!

The most segregated time in America is on Sunday morning. We have somehow neglected the greatest of all commandments love your neighbor as yourself. Yet we wonder why the church is not experiencing revival (at least to the degree that God desires). It is time for us to plug in to the power source and be energized. That power source is love. A life of miracles is the divine heritage of every born-again believer, but it must begin with loving God with all of our hearts and our neighbors as ourselves. The Bible doesn't simply say that we should love each other, but we are commanded to "walk" in love. The word *walk* comes from the Greek word *peripateo* (defined earlier), and it means "to make due use of opportunity." In other words, we have to be proactive about our love walk. God is releasing supernatural power to those who will take His message of love and reconciliation to every sphere of society. We must aggressively seek opportunities to display the love of Christ. Then and only then will we begin to walk in the power of unlimited faith and cultivate the supernatural atmosphere of heaven in every area of our lives.

FAITH AND FORGIVENESS

One day during our healing school, the Holy Spirit gave me a word of knowledge concerning people who were harboring resentment and bitterness. For about thirty minutes, I taught on the power of forgiving those who wound us. Afterward we opened the altar to pray for those who were having difficulty forgiving. To my surprise, the entire altar was filled with people. As I began to pray, the Lord impressed upon me to pray a prayer of deliverance and release over the congregation. Immediately, people cried out to God and began receiving their deliverance and freedom. In an instant, many people were physically healed.

We opened the floor for testimonies. Several people were healed of migraine headaches, chronic pain, and long-lasting infirmities. One woman traveled hundreds of miles to attend the meeting. This woman was clinically diagnosed with fibromyalgia and suffered from extreme pain for several years. She testified that during the service she was completely healed, and as we followed up with her months later, she has maintained her healing. Glory to God! Another woman was diagnosed with rheumatoid arthritis, for which she had been taking prescription steroids for years. The arthritis was so bad that her hands were balled up in knots. She went through a very devastating divorce and harbored hatred in her heart toward her ex-husband. While at the altar, she made the faith decision to forgive her husband of any and all offenses. During the next healing school, this very woman came forward to share what God did in her life. During her last doctor's appointment, the specialists were astonished because they could not find any traces of the symptoms of arthritis, nor could they find any rheumatoid in her bloodstream. From that day she was taken off all prescription medication. Hallelujah!

What was the significance of these cases? Each of the people mentioned were experiencing physical sickness in their bodies as a result of resentment and bitterness. Now, I want to clarify this point. I am not suggesting that because of their unforgiveness, they deserved sickness. I am saying that because of a refusal to walk in love toward the people in their lives, they were unable to exercise the faith necessary to receive their healing. This was a faith issue. Remember, faith works through love! When the enemy wants to attack your faith life, he will first attack your love walk. The Bible says:

> *Above all, taking the shield of faith with which you will be able to quench all the fiery darts of the wicked one* (Ephesians 6:16).

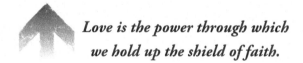 *Love is the power through which we hold up the shield of faith.*

Faith is a defensive weapon by which we resist the fiery darts of the devil. Imagine going into a battle without a shield. You will inevitably endure severe and catastrophic damage from the enemy. This is what is happening to many people in the body of Christ. They are going into battle without the shield of faith, and as a result they are undergoing spiritual, emotional, and physical attacks from the enemy. Why? You can't hold up the shield of faith and offenses at the same time. You have to make a choice. Love is the power through which we hold up the shield of faith. This is why the people I referenced earlier were unable to resist the physical attacks of the enemy on their bodies. The moment they made a conscious decision to forgive, the power of love was set into motion, and supernatural faith was released. This is why the moment they forgave they were in a position to receive their miracle.

Are you ready to receive your miracle today? Make the decision to walk in love, no matter what! It is time for you to experience all that God has ordained for your life.

FAITH DECLARATION

Father, I thank You that I have great faith in Your Word. The Bible says that faith works by love; therefore, I declare that I operate in the unconditional love of God in every area of my life. Love is Your nature. Thank You that the Holy Spirit sheds Your love abroad in my heart. I now freely forgive all those who have hurt, wounded, or offended me as an act of my free will. I release any pain, guilt, and bitterness associated with these offenses by faith in Your Word. Today, I believe that my faith operates in a greater dimension as a result of Your love for me and my love for others. In the name of Jesus, I declare that the power and presence of God are manifested in my life as I walk in love and compassion. Amen!

11

ENDURING FAITH

*My brethren, count it all joy when you fall into
various trials, knowing that the testing of your
faith produces patience. But let patience have
its perfect work, that you may be perfect and
complete, lacking nothing* (JAMES 1:2-4).

IN 1974, A FAMOUS BOXER BY THE NAME OF MUHAMMAD ALI, A.K.A
Cassius Clay, fought a young and vibrant George Foreman in the
famous "Rumble in the Jungle" bout in Zaire, Africa. Muhammad Ali was 32 years of age, and though not too old to fight in a
Heavyweight Championship match, he was much slower and more
physically limited than he was in his prime. Foreman was younger,
stronger, and faster. Most commentators predicted that Muhammad
Ali would ultimately lose the fight, and during each round this pre-
diction seemed more and more true. They did not account for one
thing—Muhammad Ali's will to win. He realized that this fight
would not be won with speed, power, and ability; he was going to
have to rely on his experience as a seasoned boxer.

During each round, Muhammad Ali would preserve energy by leaning upon the ropes and absorbing blows. This practice was later coined "the rope-a-dope." After eight rounds of absolute punishment, Muhammad Ali retaliated with every ounce of power and skill he had and ultimately managed to win by a knockout. How was he able to secure this win against a much more powerful opponent? This was only possible through something called endurance.

This is exactly what James the apostle is referring to in his epistle to the church in Jerusalem. The Bible says that our faith must be tried in order to produce patience. In the original Greek this word means steadfastness, constancy, and endurance. If we are going to operate in the power of unlimited faith, we must possess a faith that is able to endure the process of being tested. Endurance is defined as the power of enduring an unpleasant or difficult process or situation without giving way.

As a pastor and mentor, I minister to many people who are disillusioned by their trials. They are frustrated at God for "allowing" things into their lives. There are countless others who feel that the miraculous inheritance that God promises in His Word is far from being a reality for them. There is a spiritual discipline that we must adopt to ensure that we are walking in the faith that is able to withstand every obstacle and receive the manifestation of God's miraculous power; that discipline is called endurance. You may feel like you are "against the ropes," but don't give in; learn how to do a spiritual "rope-a-dope"! Wear the devil down by refusing to cave in to your feelings, emotions, or circumstances. This is what I call enduring faith. The purpose of every trial and challenge is to perfect our faith and bring us to a place of maturity and wholeness.

FAITH MUST BE TRIED!

Before we go further, I want to clear up a very common misconception; that is the notion that God causes bad things to happen to us to teach us a lesson; this is not biblical. One day, I was speaking at a church. At the end of my message, I began to speak words of wisdom and words of knowledge to the congregation. There was one particular couple I began to pray for and make prophetic decrees over. The words were very promising and encouraging. Weeks later I saw the couple at another church function, and they explained to me that since the last time I prophesied over them terrible things had taken place in their lives. The husband had an accident and severely injured himself. I was actually shocked by what the wife said next, "Don't prophesy over us anymore, because God always makes you go through stuff when He gives you a word!" I looked at this young lady with amazement. She actually believed that God was making them suffer as a result of His prophetic word for them.

 Our character is developed through obedience to God's Word (even amidst suffering) and the transforming power of the Holy Spirit.

I am sorry, but God is not schizophrenic. There is nowhere in the Bible that says God tests our character through calamity. God is omniscient; He does not need to test your character, and even if He did it would not be by calamity. Instead, the Bible says that our faith is tested. Why? Just like any muscle in your physical body, it must undergo resistance in order to develop. This resistance takes place when natural circumstances and other forces seemingly contradict what you believe to be true according to the Word of God. Our character is developed through obedience to God's Word (even amidst suffering) and the transforming power of the Holy Spirit. Faith, on the other hand, can only be developed through testing.

FAITH VS. FANTASY

It is very important for us to make the distinction between faith and fantasy. There are many people who are frustrated in the body of Christ due to the fact that what they are calling faith is actually fantasy (as we will define in a moment), and fantasy cannot stand the trial of faith no more than plastic can endure the refining fire of gold. What do I mean by the term fantasy? The word *fantasy* means the faculty or activity of imagining things, especially things that are impossible or improbable. Though there is a similar element in both faith and fantasy (the impossible), there is a drastic difference. *Faith is the spiritual power through the Word of God to manifest that which is true in the unseen realm.* Faith is not dependent on the exercise of imagination—it is based on both the written and revealed Word of God (you can use your imagination to visualize God's promises, as in the case of expectation, but that is not what we are referring to here).

Operating in unlimited faith is not a matter of fantasizing or imagining the things you desire and convincing yourself that you can have them in the future; on the contrary, faith is about standing on the solid foundation of the Word of God and choosing to believe the impossible despite contradicting evidence. Fantasy does not require any faith at all, only imagination, positivity, and optimism.

Unfortunately, there are many people in the church today who do not understand the difference between the two. There has even been a counterfeit teaching that has crept into the church, which is simply another form of New Age positive affirmation. Not to mention that many people have opened themselves to the demonic by introducing New Age ideologies into their spiritual lives. This is a very danger-ous practice that can leave a person discouraged, angry with God, and spiritually disillusioned. Real faith is based on the truth of God's Word, not just wishing and hoping what you want will happen.

DON'T LEAN ON YOUR OWN UNDERSTANDING

I can remember a time in my life when I didn't understand the difference between faith and fantasy. Many years ago, before I had a greater understanding of faith, I vividly remember a very challenging situation when my wife and I were about to lose our car. At the time I had just been laid off from my job, and we could no longer afford the car note; this was our only vehicle. The truth is that the car was never in our budget to begin with. Instead of going to God and asking Him what to do, I simply told my wife that the car would not be repossessed. I relied on optimism and positivity instead of having revelation from the Word of God. In fact, I never read a single scripture about this issue during the time. This was my dream car, and I wasn't about to lose it (at least that is what I assumed). I imagined that everything would work out just fine, because that is what "I desired."

You can imagine the look on my face when the car mysteriously disappeared from my driveway. It turned out that the bank repossessed our car. My dream turned into a nightmare. Even though things seemed like they were over, I couldn't give up because I was a man of "great faith." I went to the repo company and begged and pleaded for the release of my car, to no avail. There was nothing I could do. As I was leaving the repo yard, I found myself angry with God. "How could You allow them to take my car when I was trusting in You? The Word says that You are the Provider, doesn't it?" After my confrontation with the Lord, I heard the Holy Spirit speak a very clear word to me. He said, "Son, you never trusted Me to begin with; you were trusting in yourself. Don't blame *Me* for this situation. I had nothing to do with it!" This was like a spiritual slap in the face! The Lord was right. I trusted in my own "imagination" rather than relying on the authority and power of God's Word.

Remember, faith can only operate when the will of God is known. I was operating based on feelings and emotions, because I was ignorant of God's will. This is strictly prohibited in scripture. The Bible says:

> *Trust in the Lord with all your heart, and lean not on your own understanding* (Proverbs 3:5).

The writer of this passage uses the Hebrew word *biynah* (Strong's H998), which literally means discernment or faculty. The reason I was unable to see the manifestation of God's power in that particular situation was due to the fact that I was relying on my own "faculty" of imagination rather than the revealed Word of God. To depend on your own imagination and optimism is to "lean on your own understanding." I was operating in pride and presumption rather than biblical faith. Remember, faith is based on revelation, not presumption. After I came to this realization, I immediately repented to the Lord. My wife and I came together in prayer and began exercising faith in the Word of God. Soon after, someone called us and gave us a car, free and clear. Hallelujah! Since then, we have received several vehicles and have not financed a single one. This was a very humbling and painful experience at the time, but it taught me the difference between faith and fantasy. If it cannot withstand the test of circumstances, it is not real faith.

FAITH DOMINATES THE NATURAL REALM

Unlimited faith is the supernatural response to God's Word, which enables us to believe and experience the miraculous despite the presence of physical limitations and impossibilities. This kind of faith supersedes time, space, and even matter. We have seen this in the case of metal being transformed into bone, limbs growing, creative miracles, and supernatural multiplication. All of these things are based on spiritual realities that take precedence over the natural world. The key to possessing this enduring faith is the realization that the physical realm is subject to the spiritual realm. It does not matter how things look or feel, there is a deeper reality which holds truer and is more powerful than anything you can see, touch, taste, feel, or smell. Earlier, we made a distinction between faith and fantasy; this is not to suggest that we should not believe for the impossible, but it is important that our faith be real and genuine, as God intended. Unlimited faith is not the neglect of the natural realm, but dominion over it. To give you an example of dominion over the natural realm, I will share a brief testimony with you.

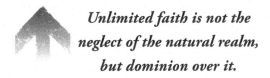

Unlimited faith is not the neglect of the natural realm, but dominion over it.

A Testimony of Faith

One night, our church was conducting an end of the year service. We only distributed a small number of invitations, and chose to rely heavily on faith and prayer. Our leadership team prayed the prayer of faith for God to bring in a great harvest. In preparation for the meeting, we purchased a very limited amount of food. Up to this time, we had not seen a large number of people in attendance in our church services. To our utter amazement, a great multitude of people filled the building. As we worshipped the Lord, His presence was almost tangible. The power of God began moving through the congregation. There were prophetic utterances and impartations of the Holy Spirit. The Glory of God manifested in a way we had never experienced before. What a wonderful time!

Several hours later, while preparing to dismiss the congregation, someone realized that we didn't have enough food to feed everyone in attendance; we barely had enough to feed our staff. Instead of panicking, we blessed the food and invited all our guests to eat in spite of the food shortage. In the natural, the food was only enough to feed about a fourth of those in attendance. The people began to eat and returned for seconds and even thirds, yet the food did not run out. The more people went to eat, the more food would literally materialize. It was amazing! Not only did the food not run out, but we had enough left over to take home, which lasted for five days. Does this sound familiar? (See Matthew 14:17-19.)

What we experienced that night is known as "supernatural multiplication" (the physical multiplication and increase of food or other resources through divine power), and we have seen it happen in many other instances. God brought the harvest of people, manifested His miraculous presence, and multiplied our food all as a result of praying in faith. This is an example of how the spiritual realm has dominion over the natural. This is a major component in exercising unlimited faith—the revelation that the Word is more powerful than anything else. If Jesus can multiply two fish and five loaves of bread, then He can also multiply chicken, fruit, Cuban sandwiches, and anything else for that matter. There are no limits to His divine power. When unlimited faith is at work, even matter doesn't matter!

MIRACULOUS CHILD BIRTH

Another example of the power that faith has over the natural realm involves several women who experienced multiple miscarriages. One in particular was so disillusioned over the loss of her previous child that she was afraid to get pregnant. When she came to us she was several weeks pregnant and anxious. Her husband refused to be excited about the current child because of the trauma of her previous miscarriage. My wife and I began to share with them the promises of God's Word according to Exodus 23:25-26, which says:

> *So you shall serve the Lord your God, and He will bless your bread and your water. And I will take sickness away from the midst of you. No one shall suffer miscarriage or be barren in your land; I will fulfill the number of your days.*

Before we shared this truth with her, she had no clue what God's will was concerning pregnancy. Remember, faith comes from the revealed Word of God (we know that the Word of God is the will of God). Until she had revelation, she could not exercise dominion over her physical circumstances. Once the revelation came, she could now place a demand on the promises of God's Word despite physical evidence, which contradicted those promises. Not only did she not have a miscarriage, she delivered a beautiful, healthy baby. I also want to mention that all three women who came to us delivered healthy babies. You see, faith makes all the difference.

 In order to see the manifestation of the miraculous power of God in our lives, we must develop a faith that endures.

Some may say, "That scripture doesn't really mean anything!" That is the problem! You will never be able to exercise dominion until you get the revelation that the Word of God is more real than anything else.

What do you believe God to do today? What miracle do you need Him to perform? He can and will do it! All He needs is for you to believe the impossible, and you will experience the miraculous.

FAITH AND PERSEVERANCE

*Therefore do not cast away your confidence, which has great reward. For you have need of **endurance**, so that after **you have done the will of God**, you may **receive the promise*** (Hebrews 10:35-36).

There is a myth in the body of Christ that being a Christian is "a walk in the park," so to speak. Though God has called us to abundant living, there will be challenges. As stated earlier, in order to see the manifestation of the miraculous power of God in our lives, we must develop a faith that endures. According to James chapter 1, our faith must be tested or proven. What happens when the thing you believe God to do (according to His Word) collides with a contradiction in the natural realm? This is what I call "spiritual turbulence." In the natural realm, turbulence takes place when an aircraft or other vessel encounters violent or unsteady movement of air. This involves the plane going through a pocket of pressure. In the case of airplanes, pilots are instructed to "press through" the turbulence until it breaks. In the same way, spiritual turbulence takes place when your faith encounters pressure (in the form of natural circumstances) that seems to contradict and/or resist the manifestation of God's promises in your life.

For instance, you are believing God for a financial miracle. The more you pray and believe that God is "Jehovah Jireh" (your all-sufficient Source), the more your bank account seems to communicate otherwise. Or you may believe God for the manifestation of the promise of healing in your life and instead of things getting better they seem to get worse. This is spiritual turbulence. What are you going to do? If you want to see manifestation, there is only one thing to do—persevere. The Bible says that we should not cast away our confidence, which has great reward (see Hebrews 10:35). Keep pushing forward into God's promise until you see the breakthrough; don't stop! Don't give up! This is not the time to take things personally or to question God's faithfulness; this is the time to persevere. This is time to endure! The Bible says:

> *Ask, and it will be given to you; seek, and you will find; knock, and it will be opened to you* (Matthew 7:7).

The Lord rewards perseverance. You must be determined to receive the promises of God for your life. We know that the Bible tells us to ask, but what does that really mean? When the Bible says ask, it uses the Greek word *aiteō* (Strong's G154), which means to "beg, crave, desire, or require." This is not a passive asking but a deliberate and diligent act of believing and receiving your request from God. The Amplified Bible translation says, "Keep on asking and it will be given you; keep on seeking and you will find; keep on knocking [reverently] and [the door] will be opened to you" (Matthew 7:7).

When it comes to the supernatural, you have to have an attitude of persistence and perseverance if you want to see the miraculous become your reality. You must continuously declare the Word of God, even if you don't see results immediately. You must continue to obey the Word of God, even when it is inconvenient. By definition, perseverance involves doing something despite difficulty, resistance, or delay in achieving success. We live in an age of instant gratification. We are taught that if something doesn't happen instantly, then it must not work.

However, the spiritual realm does not operate this way at all. There are times when you will receive an instant manifestation of the things you are praying about, but there are other times when you must exercise perseverance and determination to receive the promise. Remember, faith functions in the realm of the supernatural; therefore, faith is not limited to time and space. Jesus said that the moment we ask in prayer, believing that we receive (present tense) we shall have it (future tense) (see Mark 11:24). Notice that faith functions within the realm of the present, not the future.

FAITH SUPERSEDES TIME

You may be reading this book and wondering, "If all this is true, then why haven't I received my miracle yet?" There are so many people who have been waiting for a very long time and they have not seen a physical change in their circumstances. You might be dealing with a terminal disease or a wayward child. No matter what you are facing, you need to understand that faith supersedes time. In other words, time is not a factor when it comes to possessing unlimited faith. Why? Time is relative, while the Word of God is absolute. As you are reading this, you may be in one of several different time zones. In fact, there are at least four time zones in the United States alone. This further demonstrates the relativity of time. Faith in God is not contingent upon time. The moment you released your faith for the miracle you need, there was a shift in the realm of the spirit. To illustrate this point, I will share a biblical example found in the book of Daniel:

> And he said to me, "O Daniel, man greatly beloved, under-stand the words that I speak to you, and stand upright, for I have now been sent to you." While he was speaking this word to me, I stood trembling. Then he said to me, "Do not fear, Daniel, for from the first day that you set your heart to understand, and to humble yourself before your God, your words were heard; and I have come because of your words. But the prince of the kingdom of Persia with-stood me twenty-one days; and behold, Michael, one of the chief princes, came to help me, for I had been left alone there with the kings of Persia (Daniel 10:11-13).

Here we see that even though Daniel did not receive an angelic visitation (signifying the answer to his prayer) until twenty-one days later, the Bible says that his supplication was heard on the first day he prayed. This is amazing! This tells us that the moment we believe, something takes place in the heavenly realm. The challenge that we have is the fact that we live in the realm of time. In other words, time acknowledges the past, present, and future and regards them as a continuous reality. God does not live inside of time; He lives in the realm of the eternal. Faith draws from eternity and brings eternity into time.

Satan knows that you and I live in the physical realm, and he often attempts to exploit our perception of time in order to manipulate us into giving up on our faith. In the case of Daniel, the Prince of Persia (a demonic principality) resisted the answer to his prayer in the heavenly realm. This spiritual resistance was meant to discourage Daniel and prevent him from receiving the manifestation of God's promises in his life.

It doesn't matter how long you have been in your current circumstance, today is your day of supernatural breakthrough.

It is possible that you too may be dealing with delayed or unanswered prayers. What if I told you that God has already performed the miracle you believed Him to do? Now that you know this truth, it is time for you to press through delay and spiritual turbulence and receive your miracle today. It doesn't matter how long you have been in your current circumstance, today is your day of supernatural breakthrough. The devil doesn't count on your perseverance; it confuses him when you and I choose not to give up.

Another example of the power of unlimited faith to take dominion over the restrictions of time is found in John's Gospel. Here we see an impotent man who had been bound in that condition for thirty-eight years. Talk about a long time! Jesus asked this man one question: Will you be made whole? Once Jesus showed up on the scene, the length of his ailment became irrelevant. In John chapter 5, verse 8, Jesus said, "Rise, take up your bed and walk." Faith invites the supernatural intervention of God in the realm of time. This was the case with the impotent man. He was supernaturally restored in an instant after being crippled for thirty-eight years. Though this miracle did not originate from his faith, it required the exercise of unlimited faith to receive. The moment your faith awakens to the reality of an unlimited God, time is no longer a factor. It is time for you to receive your miracle *now!*

FAITH DECLARATION

Father, I thank You for your goodness and Your grace toward me. Today I recognize that faith is not a feeling or an emotion, it is the revelation of the truth of Your Word in my life. I declare that I have real and enduring faith. This faith supersedes time, natural circumstances, and human understanding. Right now I believe that Your Word is the final authority in my life, and through faith in Your Word I am empowered to conquer every limitation in my life. No sickness, disease, pain, or natural circumstance can stand in the way of Your miraculous promises being fulfilled in my life. These things I declare in the name of Jesus Christ. Amen!

12

THE LAW OF EXPECTATION

For we were saved in this hope, but hope that is seen
is not hope; for why does one still hope for what he
sees? But if we hope for what we do not see, we eagerly
wait for it with perseverance (ROMANS 8:24-25).

WE HAVE DISCUSSED FAITH IN GREAT DETAIL. UNLIMITED FAITH
has the ability to cause us to live in the realm of God's miraculous
power on a daily basis. In fact, faith is the "spiritual substance" that
causes the supernatural to be revealed in our lives. Each and every
believer has been called to walk as Jesus walked and to live in the
inheritance that He left the church after His death, burial, and resurrection. How else will the world know that Christ is alive and
well? We must manifest the supernatural (including signs, wonders,
miracles, and divine love) as the tangible evidence that we serve the
risen King.

There is another element that we need to understand and embrace
if this unlimited faith is going to become a reality. This element is
called expectation. In Romans 8, the Bible says that we are saved
(delivered, healed, restored, and empowered) by hope. The word *hope*

is defined as a feeling of expectation and desire for a certain thing to happen. In other words, we must have a confident expectation of something good in the future, which includes the manifestation of God's miracle power in your life. The difference between faith and hope (or expectation) is that faith operates in the present (or in the "now") while hope looks to the future. Unlimited faith is based on what God has already done, while hope is about what God will do. Faith and hope must work together in order to see the manifestation of God's power in your life—every day.

The hope that I am referring to will always manifest itself as confident expectation. In fact, expectation is a spiritual law that must be observed if we want to operate in the supernatural. As mentioned earlier, spiritual laws are the catalyst for transforming principles and precepts into living realities. We are not simply talking about legalism or methodologies. Beloved, this is so much more! We must possess expectation if we want to see miracles. The Bible says that this expectation is in the unseen (see Romans 8:24-25). The supernatural power of God first resides in the realm of the unseen, and expectation is the means by which we draw from that supernatural power. If we can see things in the natural, there is no need for expectation.

EXPECTATION BRINGS MANIFESTATION

*So he gave them his attention, **expecting** to receive something from them* (Acts 3:5).

Throughout the Bible, we see men and women of God experiencing miracles in their lives. Some received their children raised to life again, others called down fire from heaven, while others walked on water. They all have one common attribute—expectation. If you want to experience the miraculous power of God, you must learn to live in a constant state of expectancy. In the case of the man at the gate Beautiful in Acts 3, he possessed a sense of expectancy, and this expectation was the catalyst for the manifestation of divine healing in his life. Remember, expectation is the anticipation of something good or miraculous in the future. Before this man could receive his miracle, he had to posture himself in anticipation.

The dictionary defines anticipation as the act of looking forward, especially to a pleasant outcome. We have to anticipate the supernatural if we want to experience the supernatural. This practice is central to a life of miracles. We have to learn to think on the lines of the miraculous every day. We must actively anticipate the promises of God's Word manifesting in our lives. The Law of Expectation suggests that whatever you expect, you will ultimately facilitate its manifestation.

Expectation is the magnet of the spiritual realm; through expectation we attract the manifestation of God's power and promises in our lives.

Have you ever used a magnet? A magnet is usually made of iron (or some other material) and has the ability to attract other objects containing a similar substance. Growing up, we would use magnets in science class to demonstrate the power of magnetism. Expectation is the magnet of the spiritual realm; through expectation we attract the manifestation of God's power and promises in our lives. This magnetic power is displayed when you learn to set your mind on things above (spiritual realm) rather than the things on this earth (natural realm) (see Colossians 3:2). We set our mind on the realm of the Spirit by setting our mind on the Word of God. The more you and I learn to set our minds on the Word of God, the more we will expect that Word to be demonstrated in our lives. Contrariwise, if we don't have any expectation for the miraculous, we will not see the miraculous (at least not consistently).

DON'T GIVE IN TO FEAR

Also, we must be cautious to avoid negative expectations. The primary negative expectation to avoid is fear. I would define fear as the confident expectation and anticipation of evil. For example, a person says, "Things are going to go wrong today!" (a statement rooted in fear and outside of God's will), and all of a sudden things go wrong. Why? The person's negative expectation opened the door for demonic oppression and resistance, which ultimately manifested the very thing the person feared. What you anticipate you will facilitate whether the miraculous or otherwise. We build anticipation for the miraculous by meditating on the promises of God day and night. Every time you hear that promise in your spirit man, your expectation will go to another level. The Bible says:

> *So shall the knowledge of wisdom be to your soul; if you have found it, there is a prospect, and your hope* [expectation] *will not be cut off* (Proverbs 24:14).

Many people in the body of Christ are discouraged by the circumstances of their lives. They are hesitant to expect from God, because they are afraid of being disappointed. Maybe you are in this place today. Whether you are facing a challenge in your health or undergoing some other trial, the Bible says that your expectation will not be cut off (see Proverbs 24:14). In other words, your expectation will bring manifestation. Keep on expecting! Unlike faith, expectation does involve the use of imagination (as a faculty of the mind). Paul alludes to this truth in Ephesians 1:17-19:

> *That the God of our Lord Jesus Christ, the Father of glory, may give to you the spirit of wisdom and revelation in the knowledge of Him, the eyes of your understanding being enlightened; that you may know what is the hope of His*

calling, what are the riches of the glory of His inheritance in the saints, and what is the exceeding greatness of His power toward us who believe, according to the working of His mighty power.

Here Paul uses the Greek word *dianoia* (Strong's G1271) which means "the mind as a faculty of understanding or way of thinking and feeling." The Bible is telling us that our ability to exercise "spiritual expectation" or hope is directly dependent on the eyes of our understanding (or imagination) being enlightened. This joyful expectation comes from knowledge. In other words, we are only able to expect from God what we know He is capable of doing; this knowledge comes to us by revelation. This revealed knowledge produces a sense expectancy inside us.

If you want to live in expectancy, you have to learn how to see your miracle before it ever happens. Think about the miracles that you want to see in your life. Visualize yourself walking in God's miracle power. Imagine yourself healing the sick, raising the dead, and opening blinded eyes. Start to see yourself out of that wheelchair or bed of affliction. The Bible says that, "Eye has not seen, nor ear heard, nor have entered into the heart of man the things which God has prepared for those who love Him." If you can imagine it in your sanctified mind, then you know that God can do so much more.

REVELATION PRODUCES EXPECTATION

The reason why so many people in the body of Christ are not experiencing miracles is because they are not expecting miracles, and the reason why they are not expecting miracles is because they don't have revelation about who God is and what He can do. The more you come to know God's power and ability, the more you will expect the manifestation of that very power. This takes place when we come to a greater knowledge of God through the revelation of His power. This is not a mere head knowledge, but a deep revelatory knowledge that comes to us through the Holy Spirit. We see this illustrated in the case of the woman with an issue of blood. The Bible records:

> *And suddenly, a woman who had a flow of blood for twelve years came from behind and touched the hem of His garment. For she said to herself, "If only I may touch His garment, I shall be made well"* (Matthew 9:20-21).

This woman had a revelation. She knew that if she only touched the hem of Jesus's garment, she would be made well. Notice that this internal "knowing" produced an expectancy for the miraculous to take place in her life. She took her eyes off her blood condition and looked to her future with joyful anticipation, knowing that something supernatural was about to take place in her life because of Jesus. Her revelation of the power of Jesus produced an expectation on the inside of her being. She was submitting to the Law of Expectation.

We must learn to do the same! If we want to receive a miracle, we must expect a miracle. This is the spiritual law of expectation. We cannot afford to neglect this spiritual law if we want to see greater results in our spiritual lives. The more we put this law into practice, the more we will function in the supernatural.

The woman with the issue of blood knew three things that allowed her to expect a miracle. 1) She knew who Jesus was. The first thing that you and I have to do is come to the knowledge of Jesus Christ. This was a revelation of the person behind the power. 2) She knew what Jesus could do. In other words, she had a revelation of His power and ability. Without this aspect you will not be able to release your expectation. 3) She was certain of what she wanted from Jesus: "If only I may touch His garment, I shall be made well" (Matthew 9:21). This is a very important aspect of expectation. You must know what you want from God. This woman knew exactly what she wanted to receive from the Lord: to reverse her blood condition.

> *You have to make up your mind*
> *that you want more from God*
> *and more from yourself than you*
> *may be experiencing right now.*

What do you want today? Do you want to walk in the supernatural? Do you want to see the dead raised to life? Do you want to experience His miraculous provision? What you want to see will determine your expectation. You have to make up your mind that you want more from God and more from yourself than you may be experiencing right now.

This is exactly what this woman did. She seemed to be trapped in a debilitating state, yet something inside her spirit cried out for more. It no longer mattered what the doctors had to say or even what society deemed appropriate at the time; the only thing that mattered was the power of Jesus and her expectation to see that power revealed. The moment she touched Jesus, virtue (or power) was released from Him. This was the miracle working power of God (or *dynamis*). When we have revelation knowledge of the person of Jesus Christ, we can release our expectation and experience the *dynamis* (Strong's G1411) power of God in our lives.

EXPECTATION: THE ATMOSPHERE FOR MIRACLES

One night during our evening healing school, we were anticipating a great move of the Spirit of God. We had been praying for days for healings and miracles. There was a large number of people in attendance, and as more people came the atmosphere began to shift. While we were praying and soaking in the presence of God with worship, we could actually sense and see the Glory of God. Healings started breaking out instantaneously without anyone being prayed for individually. People were healed of diabetes, multiple sclerosis, chronic pain, back problems, heel spurs, arthritis, and migraines to name a few. Why was this taking place? The people came with expectation in their hearts. They were ready and willing to receive from God. This expectation literally created an atmosphere for miracles. The corporate expectation of those in attendance caused the Glory of God to manifest, and when it did miracles happened!

I often tell people that the attitude of expectation is the atmosphere for the miraculous. If you want to see miracles, cultivate an attitude of expectancy. Often, when I am preaching or teaching the Word of God, I can sense expectation. When people come into our church with a desire to encounter the presence and power of God, it literally enhances the anointing. Remember, expectation is magnetic; it draws the power of God from a human vessel or even an atmosphere. It is not uncommon for hundreds of healings to take place in our meetings before I ever teach or preach. This is a very powerful spiritual law. I believe this is one of the reasons why two people can be in the same meeting, and one will receive their breakthrough and the other does not.

Beyond faith, we must have a deliberate attitude of expectation which awaits a miracle with great anticipation. When you anticipate something, you prepare to experience it. What are you prepared to experience right now? Whatever you are prepared to experience is what you are expecting, and that is what you are going to receive. Some people are not prepared to receive anything from God and that is why they haven't received a miracle. People sometimes ask me, "Pastor, why haven't I received yet? I am in the same situation that I have always been in, and I still don't have my miracle!" The truth is that their attitude is wrong. You cannot be cynical and skeptical and still expect to receive a miracle. You must abandon yourself and aggressively expect what God says belongs to you. Stop rehearsing the pain, the delay, and the rejection. Instead, create an atmosphere (both internally and externally) of hope and expectation knowing that God is good and He longs to manifest His supernatural power in your life.

There may be a loved one you have been praying for and they still haven't experienced a turnaround. Don't let this discourage you. Start worshipping the Lord. Tell Him how good He is! Focus on the majesty and power of God in that situation. The more you concentrate on Him, the more He will reveal Himself; and when He does, expectation will rise in your inner man. This is how you create an atmosphere for the miraculous!

MAKE ROOM FOR YOUR MIRACLE

Now it happened one day that Elisha went to Shunem, where there was a notable woman, and she persuaded him to eat some food. So it was, as often as he passed by, he would turn in there to eat some food. And she said to her husband, "Look now, I know that this is a holy man of God, who passes by us regularly. Please, let us make a small upper room on the wall; and let us put a bed for him there, and a table and a chair and a lampstand; so it will be, whenever he comes to us, he can turn in there" (2 Kings 4:8-10).

One of my favorite accounts in the Old Testament is the story of Elisha and the Shunammite woman. I believe this story perfectly illustrates how you and I must be intentional about "making room for our miracle." Back in the Old Testament days, the prophets of God literally represented the Word of God in the earth. It was common knowledge that these prophets carried the presence and anointing of

God on their lives. Through this anointing they were able to manifest miracles, signs, and wonders. The Shunammite woman discerned that there was something miraculous about Elisha. She decided to make a small upper room that would accommodate Elisha whenever he decided to pass by. She was making room for the man of God and thus making room for her miracle.

This woman represents the body of Christ and that room represents an attitude of expectation. If you and I want to experience the miraculous power of God, we have to make accommodations for the supernatural in our lives on a daily basis. How do we do this? We make room for our miracle by renewing our minds. We have to change the way we think! That room represents our mind (or heart) and we accommodate the miraculous through learning to think the way God wants us to think. This includes seeing each day as an opportunity to experience the miraculous. Like the Shunammite woman, you and I have to learn to recognize divine opportunities when we see them. We have to cultivate an attitude of expectancy and position ourselves to receive everything God has for us.

We make room for our miracle by renewing our minds. We have to change the way we think!

Later in the text, we see that the Shunammite woman was approached by the prophet Elisha (through his servant Gehazi) and asked, "What can I do for you?" This is a profound question. It further demonstrates the power of expectation; because she prepared a room for the prophet, she was able to receive a miracle. The Bible says that when Elisha called the woman to his room he told her, "About this time next year you shall embrace a son." Through her anticipation of something miraculous taking place, this woman was able to conceive and give birth to a son (though her womb was barren prior to this time).

This would have been enough by itself, but the story doesn't end there. Unfortunately, her son died and now she had to make a choice. Would she mourn the loss of her son or believe that God wasn't finished yet? She chose the latter! That same attitude of expectancy facilitated yet another miracle—the resurrection of her son (see 2 Kings 4:36). There is much more that we can say about this Shunammite woman (in fact a whole book could be written about her), but the main thing to take away from her story is the power of expectancy.

Do you want to see the miraculous? You must expect the impossible! Begin to accommodate the miracle you are expecting to happen. If you are expecting a promotion, buy a new suit. If you believe God to heal those paralyzed legs, get sized for a new pair of shoes; you are about to walk! Do something you have never done before, if you want to experience what you have never experienced before. Start anticipating the supernatural power of God. This is what it means to make room for your miracle.

FAITH AND EXPECTATION

Earlier, the difference between faith and hope (or expectation) was mentioned. We learned that faith is the supernatural response to the Word of God that causes that which is in the unseen realm (based on the Word of God) to be manifested in time. Faith always operates in the present. The moment you pray in faith, you must believe that you have already received what you have prayed for—right now! On the other hand, expectation is the confident anticipation of something good in the future. Once we pray in faith, we must await the manifestation of the answer to that prayer (even though it is already done).

This requires patience. Through expectation we create an atmosphere conducive for miracles.

The truth is that faith and expectation must work together in order to experience God's power. Imagine that faith is a stick of dynamite. It is already full of latent power, which is capable of causing an explosion. If faith is the dynamite, then expectation is the match. Without something to ignite the dynamite, there will be no explosion. In the same way, without expectation you will not be able to release the power of unlimited faith. The two must work together. When faith and expectation meet, you will see an explosion of the supernatural in your life. To put it another way, faith is the main ingredient of hope or expectation and the foundation upon which it is built (see Hebrews 11:1). Faith gives substance to our expectation.

For example, you may believe God for a healing; by faith you know that you are already healed based on the authority of God's Word. Now it is time to expect the manifestation of that healing in your life. It is time to get excited about your healing miracle before it ever materializes in the natural. You must await your miracle with great anticipation. The more you expect it to manifest, the more real and tangible it will become. You must combine faith with expectation, and when you do, you will transition from imagination to manifestation.

FAITH DECLARATION

Lord, I recognize the supernatural power of expectation, and today I declare that I expect great things to happen. I have an attitude of expectation and this attitude creates an atmosphere conducive to miracles. Today I anticipate the manifestation of Your power through miracles, signs, and wonders. I declare that I am a willing vessel through whom You can reveal Your glory. Use me today to heal the sick, raise the dead, and cast out demons. I declare that the Kingdom of God has come and is manifested through me. My eyes, ears, and spiritual being are receptive to divine direction and supernatural impartations from the Holy Spirit. I am excited, expectant, and overwhelmed with joy and the thought of seeing You move on my behalf as well as others. In the name of Jesus, I declare; amen!

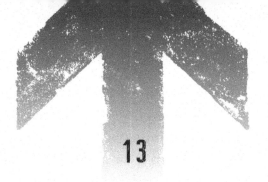

13

SPEAK THE WORD ONLY!

The centurion answered and said, "Lord, I am not worthy that You should come under my roof. But only speak a word, and my servant will be healed" (MATTHEW 8:8).

IN THE GOSPEL OF MATTHEW, WE SEE YET ANOTHER PROFOUND demonstration of the power of unlimited faith. In this account, we are told of a centurion soldier who faced a very serious problem—his servant was paralyzed and tormented. Jesus responded to the centurion's plea for help by saying, "I will come and heal him." Don't we serve a compassionate Savior? Instead of accepting Jesus's offer, the centurion responded quite to the contrary. He told Jesus that he was not worthy of such a gesture, "But only speak a Word, and my servant will be healed." This is amazing! Why did the centurion make this statement? He understood the profound power and authority of the spoken Word of God.

The centurion went further to say, "For I also am a man under authority, having soldiers under me. And I say to this one, 'Go,' and he goes; and to another, 'Come,' and he comes; and to my servant, 'Do this,' and he does it." Again, why did the centurion make these statements? He had a revelation of Jesus Christ as King and Ruler, and as a man under authority he had the ability to recognize authority when he saw it. Simply put, he recognized the power and authority of the Word of God. The words of an earthly king carry tremendous power; how much more do the words of Jesus carry omnipotent power?

After the centurion's statements, the Bible says that Jesus literally marveled. He declared, "Assuredly, I say to you, I have not found such great faith, not even in Israel!" What was so special about the centurion's statements that it would move Jesus so much? This centurion had a deep understanding of the power of faith. He understood, as we should, that faith is all about recognition. He understood that all it takes is one Word, spoken in authority, to release the supernatural.

Earlier we talked about the Law of Confession, but I want to take it even further. You need to have a revelation of the omnipotent power of the Word of God. Once you do, everything in your life will change. In the case of the centurion, he received his miracle. In fact the Bible says, "Then Jesus said to the centurion, 'Go your way; and as you have believed, so let it be done for you.' And his servant was healed that same hour." What an awesome display of the supernatural power of God. The key was to recognize the authority of the Word.

THE AUTHORITY OF THE WORD

My father was a military man, and as a result I learned military principles from a very early age. In the military it is necessary to follow orders; this is called subordination. Subordination is defined as the act of being submissive or controlled by authority. There is an expectation that those who are under authority will follow the exact instructions of their commanding officer. Jesus Christ is the Commander and Chief of the Kingdom of God, and we have a responsibility to submit to the authority of His Word. This is the key to releasing God's miracle power in your life: saying and doing what

God says, only! If we want to see results in our spiritual lives, we must develop the discipline of only speaking God's Word and nothing else.

You cannot live in the power of unlimited faith without speaking the Word.

Too many people in the body of Christ are frustrated because they refuse to conform to the Word of God. They think that they can say and do whatever they please, and things will still work out fine for them. I am sorry to tell you, but this is not true at all. By the way, I am not speaking of legalism but of recognition and obedience. The centurion in Matthew's Gospel recognized that the only thing necessary to bring about the manifestation of his miracle was the spoken Word of Jesus. We mentioned before that the Word of God is packed with miracle working power. If we want to experience this miraculous power, we must learn to say what the Word says. Notice that this involves speaking.

You cannot live in the power of unlimited faith without speaking the Word. Jesus referred to this practice as "great faith." We see several levels of faith demonstrated throughout the Gospels (little faith, mustard seed faith, and great faith). Great faith, as seen in the case of the centurion, is the highest level of faith observed by Jesus in the Gospel accounts. This faith is the faith that recognizes that the Word of God is more than enough. In another Gospel account, we see Jesus speaking to a fig tree and declaring, "Let no one eat fruit from you ever again" (Mark 11:14). The very next day, Peter noticed that the tree dried up by the roots, which Jesus cursed (see Mark 11:20-21). Peter was astonished! Why? He didn't realize that the spoken Word carried so much authority. To this Jesus responded, "Have faith in

God." This is a very powerful expression. In the original Greek it is expressed, "constantly hold and cling to the faith which resembles or possesses the nature of God." Another translation says, "Have ye the faith of God" (Wycliffe Bible). In all cases, Jesus is telling His disciples (which include us) to possess the faith that represents God's very nature and unlimited power.

Why is this so important? Unlimited faith recognizes the sovereignty of God's Word. Are you saying that God has faith? Not in the same sense as you and I have faith (belief is reserved for beings who live in time), but God does recognize the authority of His own Word (see Psalms 138). In that sense, you and I are commanded to possess the faith of God (the faith that originates from Him and acknowledges the authority and power of His Word).

WHAT ARE YOU SPEAKING?

In my many years of walking with the Lord, I have found that there is almost nothing more detrimental to the life of faith than speaking things that are contrary to the Word of God. Many years ago, I remember taking the driving examination to receive my license. Many of you may be able to remember this exam. There is a part of the exam that tests your eyesight. During this portion you are required to recite a number of letters verbatim. By saying exactly what the sheet says, you are demonstrating to the examiner that you can read and see clearly and that you are fit to drive. This exam reminds me of the life of faith in many ways. If we want to overcome the various challenges in our lives, we must learn to say only what the Word says. This does not require any creativity, only agreement and submission. The reason I believe this is such an important aspect to living in the miraculous is due to the fact that God has already laid the pattern for us to follow. We don't need to recreate anything. It has already been established for us. In fact, it is God's original design for you and me to live in the supernatural on a daily basis. To empower us to accomplish this task, God gave us His Word. All we need to do is speak the Word.

Many people believe that this is a futile exercise. They associate this type of practice with name-it-and-claim-it theology. I beg to differ! Let me ask you a question—where has speaking negativity, doubt, and fear gotten you thus far? I can tell you where—nowhere! To be more precise, it will only lead to defeatism and despair. I know because that is exactly where I was. I not only failed to experience miracles in my life, but my life was filled with stagnation and hopelessness. I often wondered how one could know what the Bible says yet not experience any real victory in their personal lives.

I suffered from lukewarm Christianity. Everything began to change in my life when I learned to say what God said (especially about me); I immediately began to experience miracles on a daily basis (I am writing from both experience and revelation). Up until that time, I felt as if I was trapped in powerless religion. You may be able to relate to this. Once you have attended the revival or conference and experienced God's power, you need something that will enable you to sustain that power daily; that something is called faith. My goal is to teach you how to use the faith God has already given you to begin living the miraculous life He always intended.

YOUR MIRACLE IS IN YOUR MOUTH

We previously defined a miracle as a surprising and welcome event that is not explicable by natural or scientific laws and is therefore considered to be the work of a divine agency. The Bible defines a miracle *(sēmeion* in the Greek) as a sign, prodigy, and portent—an unusual occurrence, transcending the common course of nature. This occurrence is designed by God to authenticate those who represent

Him. God uses miracles to cause men and women to marvel at His power. In short, a miraculous life is a marvelous life!

God wants to set us apart from the world system in which we live. How does He do this? More importantly, how can miracles become a reality for you and me? The first thing that we have to do in order to make miracles, signs, and wonders an everyday occurrence is to recognize the miracle that already dwells in our mouths. In other words, the Word of God in your mouth carries miraculous power. Earlier we spoke of the Law of Confession and the supernatural power of confessing God's Word, but I want to amplify this truth even more.

One day a young lady came into our church; she was going through a very difficult time in her life. As we ministered to her and prayed for her, she began to weep. Later we discovered that she was facing a very serious prison sentence. Once we found out, we began to pray earnestly for her. We knew by the Spirit that it was not the will of God for her to go to prison. I prayed over her and decreed that the sentence would be reversed. We declared that she would find favor in the sight of the judge and be exonerated. Weeks later, we found out that the judge reversed her prison sentence. Glory to God! That is the miracle working power of faith-filled words coming out of your mouth.

Our faith is based on the written and revealed Word of God, and once God reveals His will—we must speak with authority and purpose

I said earlier that our mouths are incubators for God's miracle power. The key is refusing to deviate from the Word of God. Stop saying what you feel, and start saying what God says. Imagine what would have transpired had we said to the young woman, "We feel so badly that you are about to go to jail for the rest of your life! Lord, Thy will be done." We would have literally pronounced a curse over her. Jesus came that we might have life and have it in abundance. That doesn't sound like a prison sentence to me. Our faith is based on the written and revealed Word of God, and once God reveals His will—we must speak with authority and purpose.

SPEAK LIFE!

It is the Spirit who gives life; the flesh profits nothing. The words that I speak to you are spirit, and they are life (John 6:63).

I truly love the Lord Jesus Christ; He is everything to me! It would be enough to worship Him for all eternity for the sacrifice of the cross, but the truth is that the cross was just the beginning. Through the sacrifice of Christ, we were empowered to become as He is and do as He did. Simply put, the cross allows us to experience the resurrection every day! When you look at the Gospels through this lens, you realize that they are more than great stories to communicate moral truths; they are manuals for supernatural living. Jesus said in the Gospel of John that the words He speaks are spirit and life (see John 6:63). We talked about the power of the Word and the Spirit, but I want to emphasize the fact that this same *life* dwells in us. We discovered that this is the Greek word *zoe*, and it literally means eternal life. I don't know who told you that your words don't mean anything, but they lied. If you are born again (born of the Spirit) you have the same *zoe* life of God inside you that Jesus had (and still has) in Himself, which He continues to possess as resurrected King (see Romans 8:11).

Just as Jesus did, you and I must release this *zoe* life through speaking. Every day you wake up you have a choice—will you speak life or will you speak death? What you choose to speak will determine your quality of life or lack thereof. This is what biblical faith is all about. Again, I am not referring to using a system to get whatever you want; I am referring to speaking the Word of God and experiencing God's will for your life. God's will is a good will! This is what the Bible says:

> Therefore do not be unwise, but understand what the will of the Lord is. And do not be drunk with wine, in which is dissipation; but be filled with the Spirit, **speaking to one another in psalms and hymns and spiritual songs, singing and making melody in your heart to the Lord,** giving thanks always for all things to God the Father in the name of our Lord Jesus Christ (Ephesians 5:17-20).

As you can see from the Word of God, we are commanded to speak psalms, hymns, and spiritual songs. The word *speak* comes from the Greek word *laleō,* which means to use words in order to declare one's mind and disclose one's thoughts. The "psalms, hymns, and spiritual songs" referred to here are not just melodic sounds, but they are declarations of God's goodness that we declare over ourselves and others based on His revealed Word. We release these declarations into the atmosphere every time we speak the promises of God aloud. In fact, I make a habit of reading the Bible audibly during my devotion time. This is a great faith-building exercise! The more I speak the Word into the atmosphere, the more things begin to shift and take the shape of what I am speaking.

This is especially true of praise and thanksgiving. I challenge you to begin praising God no matter what you are going through. You will soon discover that things are shifting in your life for your good and for His glory. My wife and I began practicing this several years ago. Once a night we would come together and pray, and once a week we would make prophetic decrees over our ministry and city. At the time, I hadn't published a single book. I didn't even know where to begin. As we continued to declare God's Word, He showed us that He wanted me to publish my first book. We didn't consult a literary agency or writing company; we just prayed and declared the promises of God. I would speak it forth and write it down.

As the Lord would reveal things, I would write them in the manuscript. Little did we know that we were birthing the vision that God placed inside us through faith-filled decrees. We declared that the book would go all around the world into several nations. In less than eight months, we received a publishing deal from a major Christian publisher for our first book. Shortly after that, our book was distributed in the United Kingdom, Italy, Germany, Canada, Africa, Asia, Australia, and the United States. Hallelujah! Everything that we spoke literally came to pass. I have written several books since then, but it all began with a decision to speak life.

What do you need to speak life to today?

YOUR WORDS ARE SEEDS

Do not be deceived, God is not mocked; for whatever a man sows, that he will also reap. For he who sows to his flesh will of the flesh reap corruption, but he who sows to the Spirit will of the Spirit reap everlasting life (Galatians 6:7-8).

I am no stranger to agriculture. In fact, my father grew up on a farm. As a young boy I remember learning how to plant cabbage and other vegetables in my back yard. I realized very quickly that I was not called to be a farmer. However, I learned a very valuable lesson: the Law of Sowing and Reaping (or Seedtime and Harvest).

This law states that whatever you sow you will ultimately reap. Simply put, whatever you plant in the ground will produce a harvest! The Bible says, "While the earth remains, seedtime and harvest, cold and heat, winter and summer, and day and night shall not cease" (Genesis 8:22). This is an irrevocable natural and spiritual law that cannot be avoided. So much so, Paul says (in his epistle to the Galatian church), "Do not be deceived, God is not mocked; for whatever a man sows, that he will also reap" (Galatians 6:7). Why does Paul use the phrase, "Do not be deceived"? The word *deceived* here comes from the Greek word *planaō,* which means to cause to lead astray, to roam, or to wander. We are told not to go astray from the spiritual law of seedtime and harvest. The truth is that we live in a culture that tells us we can sow anything we want and we won't reap; this is deception. For this reason, people say and do things that are against the Word of God, yet they wonder why they are experiencing pain and suffering. The Bible says that whatever we sow, we will inevitably reap. This is especially true of the words we speak.

YOUR WORDS WILL PRODUCE A HARVEST

Remember this, every word you speak is a seed sown that will produce a harvest. When you plant an apple seed in the ground, you don't just reap an apple; you reap an apple tree. The harvest is the exponential manifestation of the seed sown. If our words are seeds, then they have exponential power to impact our lives and the lives of those around us. So many people are reaping calamity, chaos, and destruction because of their words. On the other hand, you can reap blessing, provision, and supernatural power through the words you speak. Our words carry power. Why? We are created in the image of Almighty God. Furthermore, we have the Holy Spirit living inside (if you are born again).

The Bible says that whatever we sow, we will inevitably reap. This is especially true of the words we speak.

If you want to experience a harvest of God's supernatural power in your life, you have to develop this discipline of only saying what God says. In doing so, you will reap an exponential miraculous harvest. This is why Satan is always trying to manipulate you into saying the wrong things. He knows that you will reap the words you sow. We have a choice. We can either sow to our flesh or sow to the Spirit. What does it mean to sow to the flesh or sow to the Spirit? To sow to the flesh is to focus your time, energy, and attention on the natural. It means to gratify the carnal man. We do this by saying what we feel rather than what God says.

Every time you yield to lust, anger, pride, or disobedience, you are sowing corrupt seed into the soil of your flesh; this exercise will cause a person to reap a harvest of corruption. Contrariwise, speaking the Word of God consistently and refusing to conform to your flesh will cause the *zoe* life of God to be manifest through you; this will cause you to reap a harvest of eternal life, here and now! It all begins with the words you speak.

A TESTIMONY OF FAITH

Every year our church goes on a fast for twenty-one days. This is not a normal fast; this fast involves abstaining from negative words. For twenty-one days, we are not allowed to say anything contrary to the Word of God. This is not as easy as it seems! Especially considering the fact that we are surrounded by negativity twenty-four hours a day. Each day we choose a scriptural meditation and we speak that scripture continuously along with our regular Bible reading.

One young man in our church was uniquely tested during this time. He received a very negative report by a new manager on his job and was later reprimanded. This was very serious! Prior to this time, he never received such a negative report. Instead of being discouraged, he chose to put his faith in God and speak life over the situation. He declared that he loved his job, and that it was such a blessing to be gainfully employed. One day the new manager invited the entire department out to lunch (this is the same manager who gave him a negative report). Interestingly enough, the same manager approached him and asked if she could carpool with him. He reluctantly said yes.

While driving to the restaurant the manager asked what complaints, if any, he had about the new management staff and the department as a whole. He recalled the twenty-one days of fasting from negative words and remembered the power of speaking life. He told the manager, "I have no complaints about my department. I am just thankful to God to have a great job. Besides, I do not engage in gossip." The manager was amazed by his response. She said that his words were "refreshing!" Several days later he discovered that the same manager who gave him an extremely negative review was now recommending him for a promotion. A few weeks later, he received a promotion and a pay raise. Glory to God! The key was refusing to give in to his negative emotions, and to only say what God says!

What are you facing today? I challenge you to open your mouth and declare God's Word. I dare you to refuse to give in to your feelings. Speak the Word only, and watch the miraculous power of God manifest.

FAITH DECLARATION

Father, I declare in the name of Jesus that my words have profound power according to Proverbs 18:21. The spoken Word is that which created the visible world; therefore I take a serious inventory of the words I speak. Today I choose to speak life over every situation and circumstance that I face. I speak Your Word in faith knowing that it is full of your miracle working power. I declare that it is well with my finances, family, ministry, mind, physical body, and emotions in the name of Jesus. I release Your supernatural power by speaking Your Word now! As a result of speaking Your Word, I will reap a harvest of favor, blessing, and breakthrough. I refuse to surrender to negative thoughts, toxic emotions, fear, or anxiety. I declare that I experience supernatural manifestation and victory in my life. In the name of Jesus, amen!

14

JUST BELIEVE!

Jesus said to her, "Did I not say to you that if you would
believe you would see the glory of God?" (JOHN 11:40)

GOD DESPERATELY DESIRES TO REVEAL HIS GLORY IN THIS
generation. I believe that we are on the brink of one of the most
miraculous times in human history. Signs and wonders among the
most unlikely people will mark this season. It will not be a move
of God led by high profile preachers, but by stay-at-home mothers,
college students, teenagers, and church workers. We are going to see
widespread creative miracles, mass salvations, and notable healings
from terminal illnesses. Debts will be supernaturally canceled, and
divine resources will be released from heaven to support the global
preaching of the Gospel. All of this is available to us here and now!
What is the catalyst for this supernatural manifestation of God's
power? Just believe!

Jesus told Martha in the Gospel of John that if she would just
believe she would see the Glory of God. We mentioned that walking
by faith involved seeing into the invisible realm. If you can see the
invisible, you can believe the impossible and ultimately experience

the miraculous. Believing is the simple foundation for unlimited faith and supernatural living. In the case of Martha it was a matter of choosing to embrace a limitless God. In my many years of being a Christian, I have realized that God is looking for someone who will accept the simple truth that He is all-powerful. In fact, this is the very definition of believing: to accept something as the truth.

Let's take a moment to think about the things we accept as true. Gravity is something that we accept as true; therefore we never concern ourselves with the possibility of floating into outer space. When you accept something as the truth, you act on it with a sense of confidence. Another example is sitting on a chair. How often do you consider the fact that the chair you are sitting on could disintegrate at any moment? You don't! Why? You believe that it is sturdy and reliable. Simply put, you believe! Jesus said, "If you can believe, all things are possible to him who believes" (Mark 9:23). Do you believe that all things are possible? Do you really believe that God can do anything? This will determine what you can and cannot receive from God.

BREAKING LOGICAL BARRIERS

The story of Mary, Martha, and Lazarus addresses a serious problem in the church today. Like Martha, we have a tendency to predetermine what God can and can't do based on our limited experiences in life or what we have been taught by other people. These attitudes of doubt and unbelief have placed a glass ceiling on the modern church that God never intended.

Many of you may be able to remember the mentality you possessed in your childhood; you believed that anything was possible. Whatever your parents told you, you believed—that is, until they disappointed that belief. I can remember getting so excited when my father would tell me that he was going to pick me up early from school and take me to get ice cream. The anticipation was almost unbearable. Why? I believed what my father said!

Believing is one of the most powerful spiritual realities that exists. I often say that whatever you believe will become the force that dominates your life. To say it another way, whatever you are convinced about will ultimately take dominion over your thoughts, choices, and actions. The problem that we have when it comes to living in the miraculous is something called logic. Logic is defined as the use of reasoning based on the laws of validity. By validity, we mean the quality of being factually or logically sound. In other words, we are all taught throughout the years what is reasonable and unreasonable. The notion of miracles is absolutely ridiculous for many people. Why? They are governed by reason and logic.

We must break through the logical barrier that has kept the church trapped in intellectual excuses and spiritual powerlessness.

The Kingdom of God, on the other hand, is not governed by reason and logic; it is governed by faith and trust in God's Word. This doesn't mean that God doesn't want us to use our brain, but it does mean that the Word of God is the final authority despite facts to the contrary. In fact, we are trained our entire lives to trust in our mind. This is one of the main reasons why people are not seeing miracles, signs, and wonders in the modern church; they are too smart for their own good. We must break through the logical barrier that has kept the church trapped in intellectual excuses and spiritual powerlessness. We have replaced the power of God with seminary degrees and religious philosophies (though there is nothing inherently wrong with seminary).

The people who Christ ministered to did not have the luxury of logic as we do today. They did not have time for reasonable explanations and factual observations; they were desperate for the power of God. Imagine for a moment a person who has been crippled from birth being supernaturally healed in an instant; is there any logical explanation for that? If you and I want to enter into the realm of impossibilities we have to move beyond reason into childlike faith and belief. We must embrace God's truth above any and all facts. We have to literally become foolish enough to trust God.

THE FOOLISHNESS OF GOD

Because the foolishness of God is wiser than men, and the weakness of God is stronger than men. But God has chosen the foolish things of the world to put to shame the wise, and God has chosen the weak things of the world to put to shame the things which are mighty (1 Corinthians 1:25,27).

One very important component to your ability to walk in the power of unlimited faith is an understanding of the "foolishness of God." Often I am asked, "Why are people seeing more miracles, signs, and wonders in third world countries than we are in the Western world?" Are people in other countries more powerful and more anointed than they are where you live? The truth of the matter is that it has very little to do with geography and very much to do with attitude. The Bible says if you will believe, you will see the glory of God. It is an issue of belief! It is really that simple!

Unfortunately, many people have unknowingly embraced a mindset of skepticism and doubt. This mentality can neutralize your ability to believe God for the miraculous. The Bible says in 1 Corinthians chapter 1 verse 25 that "the foolishness of God is wiser than men."

What does this mean? First of all, the word *foolishness* here comes from the Greek word *moros* (Strong's G3466), which means foolish or unwise. This is where we derive the English word *moron*. A moron is a stupid person. I know this may seem like a serious insult, but Paul the apostle is speaking in oxymoronic language. God is incapable of any stupidity or foolishness; however, His principles and precepts appear foolish to the world system.

For instance, the world system tells us to rely on our own wisdom to solve problems in our lives. The Word of God tells us not to lean on our own understanding. These are two totally contradictory perspectives. The point is that God's way of doing things violates the laws of reason and logic. This is what the Bible calls the "foolishness of God." This is an attitude that takes God at His Word, no matter how foolish or stupid it seems. I am reminded of Peter walking on water; an apparently foolish concept in the natural realm. He decided that his desire to be with his Lord was more important than the laws of gravity, and through the supernatural power of believing, gravity itself was suspended. The moment Peter looked to natural circumstances, reason and logic kicked in and he nearly drowned.

There are many people today who are "drowning" in a sea of doubt, unbelief, skepticism, and fear. The moment you make the decision to look to Jesus (as Author and Finisher of your faith), you will walk above the circumstances of this life and operate in a dimension of the miraculous that you have yet to conceive or imagine. The question is: will you be foolish enough to believe? Stop listening to the logical excuses of the enemy. Make up in your mind and heart that you will go all the way with God.

PULLING DOWN STRONGHOLDS

*For the weapons of our warfare are not carnal but mighty
in God for pulling down strongholds, casting down*

arguments and every high thing that exalts itself against the knowledge of God, bringing every thought into captivity to the obedience of Christ (2 Corinthians 10:4-5).

The truth is that you and I are in a battle—not a battle in the physical realm, but in the mind. The thoughts, ideas, and influences we yield to will determine who wins and who loses. The Bible says in the book of 2 Corinthians that the weapons of our warfare are not carnal, they are mighty (powerful) through God. In other words, we can't fight this spiritual and mental battle with physical weapons. If we are going to experience the miraculous power of unlimited faith we have to address the enemies of this objective.

Whether you realize it or not, the biggest opponents of faith and the supernatural in general exist in your own mind. The Bible commands us to "pull down strongholds." What does this mean? In the original Greek, this literally means to demolish and destroy fortresses. Paul is using military language to describe the battle of the mind. Just like in a physical war, the person who takes the high ground has a strategic advantage in the battle. If you want to win the battle, you must first penetrate and demolish the fortresses of your enemy. In the same way, you and I have to take dominion over our thought life and pull down mental strongholds.

The Bible goes further to say that we are to cast down "arguments" or "imaginations." This is the Greek word *logismos,* which means reckonings, computations, and reasoning hostile to faith. The idea that Paul is conveying is that the strongholds he refers to are logical arguments and reasonings that establish themselves as mental fortresses. For example, God says that He wants to heal you of a terminal illness; a thought comes and says, "That will never happen!" Though this may seem like a normal response, it is really an insidious ploy of the enemy to keep you away from your miracle. The Bible says that we must pull down these arguments in our mind. We must bring these thoughts, which exalt themselves above your knowledge of God, into captivity. This can only happen when you meditate on the Word of God and allow Him to create a new framework for the impossible. In other words, you need to lose your mind—the carnal mind that is. Approach God like a three-year-old child who believes every word his or her father speaks. Refuse to accept the logical reasons why you can't walk in the miraculous and simply "step out on the water" in faith.

 Approach God like a three-year-old child who believes every word his or her father speaks.

A TESTIMONY OF FAITH

One night I was ministering at a church on the Law of Expectation. I began to encourage the people to take the limits off of their perception of what God could do and simply believe the impossible. The more I taught, the more I literally felt the people's expectation rise. I began to flow in words of knowledge and wisdom (expectation places a demand on gifts of the Spirit). I said that there was a woman present who was currently involved in an abusive relationship and there were countless others who had been touched by God's healing power. I said that countless others were being healed of anxiety, depression, and mind-binding spirits. I asked the congregants to come forward and testify of their healing and deliverance.

After much entreaty, no one came up to testify. Instead of moving on, I refused to relent. I knew that God was ready to perform miracles that night. One lady reluctantly came forward. At first she refused to speak. I urged her to share and comforted her in the fact that no one would judge or criticize her. She confessed that she was the woman in an abusive relationship and that she was battling anxiety and fear. She also said that the anxiety was created by the discovery of a lump near the right side of her breast. In fact, she had two previous lumps that had to be medically addressed. I began to curse the lump in her breast area and release the fire of God to consume anything that was unclean in her body. I declared that she would not die, but live.

She began to weep in the presence of God. After I was done praying for her, she went back to her seat and examined the area between her breast and underarm. To her amazement, she could not find the lump anymore. The lump completely dissolved under the fire of God. Hallelujah! God is the same yesterday, today, and forever! Is there anything He cannot do? If we will dare to believe, we will see the glory of God revealed in our lives. The key is to cast down logical arguments, reasoning, and analytical strongholds that try to talk you out of the miraculous. You too can experience miracles. You can walk in the supernatural on a daily basis. All you have to do is *believe!*

FAITH DECLARATION

Father, I declare in the name of Jesus Christ that I have childlike faith. I am a believer in Your Word. Nothing is impossible to those who believe; therefore, I cast down every thought, argument, imagination, and logical explanation that would attempt to contradict Your Word. I declare that Your Word is the final authority in my life. I believe the impossible, I see the invisible, and I experience the miraculous in my life from this day forward. Thank You for the faith and courage to break through every logical barrier that exists in my life. I renounce fear, skepticism, and doubt, and I decree that I am full of faith and love. Today I declare that the miraculous has become my new normal. In Jesus's name, amen!

15

UNLIMITED FAITH

We are bound to thank God always for you, brethren,
as it is fitting, because your faith grows exceedingly,
and the love of every one of you all abounds
toward each other (2 THESSALONIANS 1:3).

WE HAVE DISCOVERED THUS FAR THAT GOD HAS INVITED US INTO a life of miracles. No matter where you are or what you may have encountered up to this point, you can experience this miraculous transformation. Every person who reads this book can walk in the supernatural power of God. All it takes is a decision to possess unlimited faith in God's Word—the source of God's miracle working power.

You may be thinking to yourself, "It can't be this easy!" Well, it is this easy! The most profound things in life are simple, and this is why people have a tendency to overlook them. Years ago I was in the same predicament that some of you may be in currently. I knew the Bible, attended church regularly, gave tithes, et cetera, but there was something missing. The things I read about in the Bible did not seem to hold completely true in my life. There was incongruence between that which was written and that which was realized. In fact, I believe the vast majority of people in the Western church are in this same place. Studies have shown than nearly 60 percent of all Christians in the United States are cessationists (believing that the gifts of the Spirit are no longer available today). This would explain much of the powerlessness that you see in our modern churches.

We have replaced Spirit-filled preaching with motivational messages that encourage people to see God as a vending machine rather than King. The power and demonstration of the Holy Spirit (signs, wonders, and miracles) has been replaced by cutting edge public relations and high-tech marketing strategies. We attempt to woo the un-churched with family friendly activities, church coffee shops, and other religious entertainment. Yet there is a cry throughout the land. People want to experience the supernatural. The church holds the key to this dimension of God's glory.

Through the pages of this book, practical keys have been revealed to walking in the power of unlimited faith. We have discovered that we must invest ourselves in God's Word, develop the discipline of seeing the invisible, and cultivate the "hearing of faith," to name a few things. The question still remains: what does it mean to walk in unlimited faith?

Paul thanked God for the Thessalonian church. He noted that their faith grew "exceedingly." This is the Greek word *hyperauxanō* and means to increase beyond measure. In other words, this is a faith without bounds or limits. The Thessalonians are a spiritual prototype for modern-day believers in Jesus. God wants the same to be said of us. He desires a faith without limits, restrictions, barriers, or hindrances. A faith that is childlike in expression, but Godlike in substance.

Beloved, this is the simple key to experiencing the miraculous on a daily basis. We, like the church of old, can be spiritual prototypes for the generations to come (if the Lord tarries). Unlimited faith is a faith that refuses to accept the lie that God has somehow changed or has less power than when the Bible was written.

GOD'S LIMITLESS POWER

The eyes of your understanding being enlightened; that you may know what is the hope of His calling, what are the riches of the glory of His inheritance in the saints, and what is the exceeding greatness of His power toward us who believe, according to the working of His mighty power (Ephesians 1:18-19).

Do you believe that God can do anything? Are you completely convinced that He is omnipotent? The basis for unlimited faith is a revelation of God's limitless power. This is a central theme throughout the Bible, yet we seem to forget it at times. Paul reminds us in the book of Ephesians. In the first chapter of Ephesians, Apostle Paul prays a prayer over the church that the "eyes of their understanding" will be enlightened, that they might know the riches of God's glory and the "exceeding greatness of His power toward us who believe." I want to focus on this statement (the exceeding greatness of His power toward us who believe). What is the "exceeding greatness of God's power"?

 *The basis for unlimited faith is a revelation of God's limitless power.*

First let us define the word *exceeding*. This is the Greek word *hyperballo*, which means to transcend, surpass, excel, or to throw over, and beyond anything. This is a very loaded definition. This definition suggests that the power of God transcends and surpasses anything that we can comprehend or imagine. Of course the word *power* is the word *dynamis,* which means the power for performing miracles. When we combine these definitions, we see that God's ability to perform the miraculous exceeds any natural limitation that exists. This power has to be revealed to us by the Holy Spirit. This is why Paul prays that the eyes of our understanding would be enlightened. This is how it is written in the Amplified Version:

> *And [so that you can know and understand] what is the immeasurable and unlimited and surpassing greatness of His power in and for us who believe, as demonstrated in the working of His mighty strength* (Ephesians 1:19).

We must know and understand (by revelation) the "immeasurable and unlimited and surpassing" greatness of God's power (ability to perform miracles). This is such an awesome truth! However, there is a part of this verse that we have a tendency to overlook: "to us who believe." This awesome power can only be experienced by those of us who believe (accept this biblical reality as truth). Faith is the key to releasing this miracle working power of God. It is never a question of God's ability or His willingness; it is always a question of our willingness to believe.

If we will simply accept, by faith, that God can really do anything, we will experience the fullness of His power on a daily basis. I don't know about you, but that sounds good to me. Imagine for a moment a life filled with endless possibilities. Imagine praying over your children and seeing them saved, healed, and delivered. Imagine being the go-to person in your community for the miraculous. All of this and more are available to us once we remove the mental blockers, religious barriers, and anything else that stands in the way of us trusting God without limitations. If God is a God of unlimited power, then we ought to be people of unlimited faith.

SUPERNATURAL MIND RENEWAL

I beseech you therefore, brethren, by the mercies of God, that you present your bodies a living sacrifice, holy, acceptable to God, which is your reasonable service. And do not be conformed to this world, but be transformed by the renewing of your mind, that you may prove what is that good and acceptable and perfect will of God (Romans 12:1-2).

The truth is that the supernatural does not come *natural* to us. Ever since Adam fell in the Garden of Eden, man became bound to the natural realm. In other words, we have focused on what we can see, taste, hear, feel, and smell. In order to begin living in the miraculous, we have to exercise unlimited faith, and this requires supernatural mind renewal. What is meant by the term supernatural mind renewal? In the 12th chapter of Romans, we are exhorted by God to present our bodies as living sacrifices and to not be conformed to this world, but rather be transformed by the *renewing* of our minds. The word *transformed* is the Greek word *metamorphoō* and it means to change into another form, to transform, or to transfigure. This is the same word found in the Gospel of Mark chapter 9, verse 2:

*Now after six days Jesus took Peter, James, and John, and led them up on a high mountain apart by themselves; and He was **transfigured** before them.*

During this transfiguration, Jesus took on a glorified persona. He began to display the brilliance and glory of the heavenly realm. The disciples were so impressed by this supernatural transformation that they requested to build tents on this mountain of transfiguration—one for Jesus, and two others for Moses and Elijah (see Mark 9:5). This is what Paul is alluding to when he commands us to "be transformed." In other words, God is calling you and me to take on the persona of the heavenly realm rather than the natural realm. We are to display the glory of God by living a supernatural lifestyle.

How do we experience this transformation or transfiguration? We can only be transformed by the renewing of our minds. The word for renew in Romans 12 is the Greek word *anakainōsis,* which means a renovation or complete change for the better. When you think of the word *renovation,* you probably think of a building being renovated. In order to renovate a building, you must tear down old walls and infrastructures and erect new ones. Earlier we mentioned that the supernatural is not something that comes natural to us. We have to be retrained and rewired to walk in the supernatural. We said that meditating on the Word of God is a vital component to this mind renewal.

The more we read, meditate on, and speak the Word of God, the more we began to transform into the image of Jesus Christ. This is what I call a "supernatural paradigm shift." Human beings are creatures of habit; therefore we have to renounce old habits and adopt new ones. We have to divorce ourselves from wrong thoughts and wrong emotions and embrace the mind of Christ. As we allow the Holy Spirit to make us more like Jesus, we will begin to do as He did. This is what it means to experience supernatural mind renewal. In renewing our minds, we will become demonstrators of God's miraculous power. It is the will of God for every believer in Jesus to walk in the supernatural.

 The more we read, meditate on, and speak the Word of God, the more we began to transform into the image of Jesus Christ.

JESUS: THE AUTHOR OF OUR FAITH

*Looking unto Jesus, the **author** and finisher of our faith,*
who for the joy that was set before Him endured the cross,
despising the shame, and has sat down at the right hand
of the throne of God (Hebrews 12:2).

One of the common misconceptions that exists in the church (which we began addressing in an earlier chapter) is the idea that we have to have a special kind of faith to experience the miraculous. The truth is, we already have divine faith, because God gave it to us as a gift. In fact, the Bible says that we have been crucified with Christ, and the life we currently live we live by faith in the Son of God (or the faith of God's Son, Wycliffe Bible) The idea is that we no longer live by our own faith, we live by the faith God gave us in Christ. Now I want to clear up another misconception. There is something called the gift of faith, which we see in 1 Corinthians 12:7-9:

> *But the manifestation of the Spirit is given to each one for*
> *the profit of all: for to one is given the word of wisdom*
> *through the Spirit, to another the word of knowledge*
> *through the same Spirit, to another faith by the same*
> *Spirit, to another gifts of healings by the same Spirit.*

We can clearly see from scripture that there is such a thing as the gift of faith, which is the supernatural manifestation of the Holy Spirit that enables a person to believe God in an audacious and abnormal way in certain instances. The gift of faith goes far above and beyond the normal range of miracles (compared to others in the church). This has nothing to do with the person, but it is solely based on the manifestation of the Spirit for the collective profit of the body of Christ. This manifestation of faith usually accompanies one of the power gifts listed in 1 Corinthians 12 (words of wisdom, words of knowledge, prophecy, and healing). This gift is meant to provoke the church to a greater level of confidence in God.

For example, when the Lord gives a prophetic word to a man or woman of God to speak, there must be a supernatural boldness that accompanies that Word, or when a person has no legs and supernatural boldness comes to a minister to manifest a creative miracle—this is the gift of faith. However, this has nothing to do with the capacity Jesus Christ has given every believer to walk in the supernatural consistently. We all have the faith for miracles! If we didn't, Jesus would not have said, "these signs shall follow *them who believe*," which includes speaking in tongues, casting out demons, and healing all manner of sickness. We don't have to wait for "the gift of faith," we can move in the miraculous right now! Jesus is the Author of our faith. This literally means that He is the Source of our faith and the example of trust in God that we are called to follow. He was able to manifest the power of God because He always looked to the Father and not Himself.

In the same way, we must look to Jesus and not the natural limitations imposed on us by this world system. The faith God has given us must be developed. This takes practice and mind renewal. The more you exercise your faith in the Word of God, the more your capacity for the miraculous will grow.

ABUSES OF FAITH

I want to take a moment and briefly address some abuses of faith that we have seen in recent years. I have personally experienced many of these abuses of faith while teaching and understand the confusion and pain that they can cause. The main abuse I have seen is the counterfeit manifestations of faith we have seen in many circles of Christianity. These include:

1. *The promotion of materialism, greed, and covetousness in the name of faith.*

This practice is extremely detrimental to the body of Christ. I have seen people literally shipwreck their faith as a result of this wrong practice. I can remember a friend of mine who would put a picture of a Bentley on his wall and confess that he owned a Bentley "in Jesus's name!" He would wake up every morning and say, "I receive my Bentley, I receive my Bentley, and I receive my Bentley!" It took all his time and energy. Needless to say, he never "received" his Bentley. Though I believe in biblical prosperity, I am cautious to avoid such extremes. This person barely had a job, yet he was asking God for a Bentley. Why? The church he attended promoted this type of behavior. They taught that if you didn't drive a Bentley or Rolls Royce, you were unsuccessful. Beloved, this is absolute foolishness. That same young man ended up in a backslidden state. Again, I want to reiterate that there is nothing inherently wrong with desiring or owning a luxury vehicle, but when material possessions become the focal point of our faith, it can become a detriment to our spiritual lives. The ultimate focus of our faith should be Christ and His Kingdom. Be cautious of practices rooted in the lust of the flesh.

 Remember, real faith cannot exist outside of an intimate relationship with God.

2. *The use of God's Word as a means to get whatever you want.*

This is also an extremely dangerous practice because the Bible says, *"After these things the word of the Lord came to Abram in a vision, saying, 'Do not be afraid, Abram. I am your **shield**, your exceedingly* *great reward'"* (Genesis 15:1). The Bible says that He is our reward. This means that we are not to seek God only for the things He gives us. God is not Santa Claus; He is King and Lord. The Bible also says that we are to approach Him out of love and reverence. God does bless us—in fact, He is obligated to do so under the New Covenant—but if we only approach Him for material things then we are not seeking Him first. Remember, real faith cannot exist outside of an intimate relationship with God. Imagine only going to your parent or spouse when you needed money; that person would feel used. Many Christians are unknowingly operating in the realm of witchcraft because they are manipulating "the Word" to fulfill selfish desires. This includes ministers giving false prophetic words for financial gain. This grieves God's heart. He wants us to love Him for who He is, not just what He does. Seek first the Kingdom of God, and all these things will be added to you (see Matthew 6:33).

3. *"You don't have enough faith!"*

This is probably one of the worse abuses I have seen in the church. When people are told that they are sick, suffering, and even dying because they don't have enough faith, they are driven to a state of mental and emotional anguish. They begin to question whether or not God loves them. Again, many people are not living by faith, and as a result they are unable to receive many blessings and provisions, but to beat someone down spiritually and emotionally is outright abusive. Jesus is the Author and Finisher of our faith. It is not about your faith—it is about His faith operating in you. You already have the faith that you need to receive any blessing or miracle from God. Never allow someone to tell you that you don't have enough faith. You simply need to learn how to use what you already have to receive that which He has graciously prepared for you.

LIVING IN THE MIRACULOUS *EVERY DAY!*

In short, God has called you and me to live a miraculous life. This miraculous life includes walking in God's supernatural power on a daily basis, seeing the sick healed, the lame walk, the dead raised to life, supernatural provision, and the manifestation of God's Kingdom, here and now. God wants to use you to display His goodness and to bring reconciliation to a lost and dying world. He wants you to demonstrate the power and reality of His Kingdom through signs, wonders, and miracles. This calling is not just for the elite, but also for all who will embrace it.

We have discovered through the pages of this book that the secret to releasing this miraculous power on a daily basis is "unlimited faith." We are living in the greatest time in human history, and we have a tremendous opportunity to display God's glory to this generation. Can you really live in the miraculous every day? The answer is YES! There was a time in my life when this seemed so farfetched. I felt as if I was a window shopper or a spectator. One day everything changed when God opened my eyes and revealed to me that He had set an open door before me. This was a door to the supernatural life. This door was His Word—and faith was the key. In that moment, just like you, I had a choice. Would I settle for lukewarm Christianity or would I reach for more? I made the decision to live in God's power. This was a decision to walk by faith and not by sight.

Today is your day to make the same decision. Today is the day for you to experience the miraculous. Release your faith now and begin operating in the realm of the spirit. This is your divine inheritance! All you need to do is believe. If you will believe God by faith, you will see His glory, here and now!

Pray this prayer with your whole heart (aloud):

Father, in the name of Jesus Christ I thank You for Your unlimited power. Right now I make the decision to walk in my divine inheritance in Christ. From this day forward, I will walk in "unlimited faith" and release Your supernatural power in every area of my life, including my prayer life, relationships, ministry, finances, and health. I declare that I am full of faith. I let go of every spiritual, mental, and emotional weight that I have carried. I refuse to embrace any more excuses. I will walk as Jesus walked and do as Jesus did. Today is my day to live in the miraculous! In Jesus's name. Amen!

ABOUT THE AUTHOR

At the tender age of 15, Pastor Kynan committed his life to Jesus Christ and was subsequently filled with the Holy Spirit. After getting involved in his local church, God made His call manifest to Kynan audibly. For many years, Kynan served in the local church and was involved with various ministries. After running from the call of God, he was finally arrested by the Holy Spirit. Several years ago, the Lord told Kynan to begin a teaching ministry in Tampa, Florida. At this point, the vision for Grace & Peace Global Fellowship was birthed.

> *For if by one man's offense death reined by one; much more they which receive abundance of grace and of the gift of righteousness shall reign in life by one, Jesus Christ* (Romans 5:17).

He says this about his ministry:

Romans 5:17 is the vision and mission of our ministry—to see the person, power, and presence of Jesus Christ manifested in the lives of people everywhere that they might reign in life. Through this ministry we desire to see millions of souls saved and restored through the Gospel of Jesus Christ. We accomplish this mission by proclaiming the unadulterated, life changing Word of God. Our outreach ministry serves as the catalyst to spread this message. Every week we provide resources to people so that they might become more conscious of Christ's love for them and enter into the fullness of His finished work and thereby be positioned to walk in their God-ordained assignment, namely the Great Commission as outlined in Matthew 28:19.

Our weekly podcast (FaithTalk) serves as a platform to discuss various issues in the body of Christ and the world and shed light on those issues through the illumination of God's Word. We are committed to spreading the Gospel through our preaching ministry, speaking engagements, teaching resources, and Internet and media platforms.

To date, we have reached countless numbers of people with the Gospel. Through the combined efforts of our weekly outreach ministry and new media resources, we have exposed thousands to the Gospel of Grace every week. Currently we are communicating God's Word to people in North America, India, Haiti, and Nigeria. We are engaging in several outreach efforts, which have a global impact.

Pastor Kynan is committed to allowing the power and anointing of the Holy Spirit to flow through him and touch God's people. He is a committed husband to Gloria and mentor and father to two beautiful daughters, Ella and Naomi, and handsome son, Isaac.

For information on booking a presentation, for prayer requests, or to support this ministry, write to or call:

Kynan Bridges Ministries

PO BOX 159

Ruskin, FL 33575

Phone: 1.800.516.7038

Or visit us at: www.kynanbridges.org